Buildings in the Yorkshire Dales

Who built them, when and how?

by

Arthur Raistrick

Dalesman Books

1981

The Dalesman Publishing Company Ltd.
Clapham (via Lancaster), North Yorkshire
First published 1976
Reprinted 1981

ISBN: 0 85206 367 9

Printed by Waddington & Sons (Printers) Ltd., Fielden Square,
Todmorden, Lancashire

Contents

The cover photographs show:— Front: Town Head, Malham (Tom Parker); Back: Countersett Hall (G. Bernard Wood). All unacknowledged photographs in the text (pages 33-40 and 65-72) are by the author.

Preface

VISITORS to the Dales soon become attracted by houses and cottages of the seventeenth and eighteenth centuries with the mullioned windows which guide books label "traditional" and which can be seen in many of the villages. These however are only a small proportion of the village buildings, many of which are plainer and smaller. Nonetheless, most villages attain a pleasing unity and a character which at once distinguishes them as belonging in the Dales. This may in part be due to the village plan and setting, to the building materials and to some constructional details. This book is aimed to be an outline history of when, how and why they came to be built. Where did the varying styles come from? How did the Dales people who made these various buildings set about the work of design, getting together the materials, putting up the building and so on? More attention will be paid to the people concerned with making, living in and using them than to architectural merit.

The area chosen is that generally called the Yorkshire Dales and which includes the whole of the Dales National Park, with some small additions and Nidderdale on the east side. This is the country lying between Airedale and Stainmore, going on the west as far as the Lune-Rawthey valley and on the east to a less definite line which approximates to one from Barnard Castle by Richmond, Ripon and Harrogate and then across to Skipton.

There is already an abundance of guide books and descriptions of the Dales for the information of the tourist so that aspect of them can be ignored or treated in outline only. It will be useful to start with some brief remarks on the geology if we are to understand and appreciate the abundance and variety of building materials which have been available in the Dales. In the nineteenth century a large quarrying industry became an important source of employment and much stone was exported by rail to the growing industrial towns of East Lancashire. That is a separate story and in this book the quarrying will be limited to the purely local needs supplied in part from the township quarries designated later by the various Enclosure Awards. A few larger quarries supplied special quality stone for larger buildings.

A village originated as a living organism, a community of people working within a restricted area and making its own shelter and providing for that of its animals. Through the centuries the communities have grown in numbers of inhabitants and so in complexity and new buildings have been added from time to time, usually in keeping with changing social conditions and fashions. In the present century these additions have had less relation to the countryside than was the case during all the previous centuries of growth. Now the population is being invaded by townsfolk, either retiring or seeking a "second home" for holiday purposes. Village communities are now very much a mixture of rural and urban folk and ideas. If the character of the villages which has made them so attractive in the recent past is to be kept to a reasonable extent, a sympathetic and knowledgeable understanding of their growth will help and it is hoped that this study will contribute to promoting such an understanding.

The ideas advanced are the author's own, drawn from a lifetime's knowledge and love of the area, and from the experience of generations of Dales forebears which, through grandparents' and parents' talk and teaching in the most impressionable years of youth, was passed on in unforgettable form.

LINTON
1976.

1. Geology and Building Materials

GEOLOGICALLY the area contains rocks of varied age, the oldest being in the south-west. In the Ingleton Glens of Kingsdale and Chapel-le-Dale there is a long series of rocks so moved and folded that they stand nearly vertically on edge and many beds are probably repeated by concertina folding. The Ingletonian Series as these are called was for long regarded as being of pre-Cambrian age, deposited before the periods when there was life on the earth, and among the oldest known rocks. Some recent researches however have questioned this and it is now suggested that they may be much younger. For our purposes their importance is that where they are exposed beneath the limestones they show a long succession of bands of grit and slate more than a mile long. Some of the bands of grit and all the bands of slate have been quarried in the past for building materials. On entering the Glens from Ingleton above the Meal Bank Quarry, which is in limestone south of the great Craven Fault, the path goes between two large quarries which are in the first of the slate beds, one each side of the stream. Another large slate quarry makes the broad space at the lower end of the Baxengill Gorge and other quarries are seen in the Twistleton Glen which extends below Thornton Force. These slates have been used in the Ingleton area, over a large part of this south-west region of the Dales and in adjacent parts of Lancashire. Slates of the same possible pre-Cambrian age were also quarried in Ribblesdale from a huge hole in the floor of the present Horton-in-Ribblesdale limestone quarry. This old slate quarry is now flooded but its vast size makes one realise that these rocks must have had a considerable influence on buildings put up during its active life in the nineteenth and early twentieth centuries.

Above the Ingletonian Series there is a geological gap and the next rocks which are seen in the valleys of Crummackdale, Ribblesdale below Horton and in a small patch at Malham Tarn, belong to the Ordovician and Silurian systems. The Silurian is the one that has provided vast quantities of building materials.

8

The Silurian rocks here have four subdivisions—some shales, the Austwick Grits, the Horton Flags and the Studfold Sandstone. All these except the shales have been quarried for building stone and today they form part of the most quarried area of the Dales, though now, regrettably, these splendid rocks are being broken and crushed for roadstone and concrete aggregate. These rocks cross the valleys under the limestone, lying in broad belts in a big down-fold or syncline running a little to the south of west to east, and revealed in Crummackdale above Austwick and in Ribblesdale between Stainforth and Horton, where erosion has removed the limestone. The Studfold Sandstone makes the centre of the syncline and because of its dip to the east does not reach into Crummackdale. It lies in a wide area on the east of the Ribble making the high hummocky ground round Studfold just above Helwith Bridge. Here some quarries can be seen in it, and it is also exposed in many outcrops. It lies in an elongated basin of Horton Flags, the nose of which just extends into the west side of Crummackdale. There are some very obvious quarries on the east side of the dale, just under the limestone scars. The largest quarries in the Horton Flags were those at Helwith Bridge, and through the seventeenth, eighteenth and nineteenth centuries these flags were widely used in Ribblesdale, carried over into Littondale and spread west and south-west over a wide part of Craven and the Lancashire border country. The flags were got in many large sizes and in thicknesses from an inch to a foot or more. Much of the thicker stuff was cut up for building stone, while the largest thinner flags were used to make rain-water tanks, some of which can still be seen at Dales farms. Many of the seventeenth century farms still have dairies with Horton Flag shelves and some dairies and kitchens are still floored with them. The floors are a deep blue colour, wonderfully smoothed by the use in past years of sharp sand and the old-fashioned sand mop—a large block of sandstone mounted with a broom handle set at an angle, with which the sanded floor was scrubbed. Horton Flags can also be seen in gateposts and in some of the older clapper bridges.

The Austwick Grits are mainly a massive sandstone which has provided excellent building stone, but there are also a few beds of finer slate among them which were formerly quarried for roofing slates. The chartulary of Fountains Abbey mentions the slate quarry of Gospatric at Austwick in the thirteenth century. To the west of the Dent Fault, which runs down the east side of the Rawthey valley and through Barbondale, the Howgill Fells are made of rocks of the Silurian age but there they are more slaty and soft and, with other and better rocks close at hand, fortunately they have not been quarried.

The rest of the Dales area is made of rocks belonging to the

Carboniferous system. There are four divisions from the lowest upwards—the Great Scar Limestone, the Yoredale Series, the Millstone Grit and the Coal Measures. The Coal Measures only occur in the small area of the Ingleton coalfield brought down by the Craven Fault. The only building material in this is the bricks made from some of the shale which makes up the greater part of the measures—a big old brick kiln can be seen just below Meal Bank Quarry. There is an effective dip of all the strata towards the north-east so that the Great Scar Limestone, which is the dominant rock of the scenery of the south-west from Settle to Grassington is gradually buried under the Yoredale and is only seen in the bottom of the Wensleydale valley. The Yore-dales reach their maximum development in Wensleydale — Yoredale, from which they take their name. To the east and north-east the Millstone Grit becomes dominant and from being seen only as a tiny cap on the summits of Ingleborough and Penyghent it increases in area until it makes the extensive moors from Rumbalds Moor between Aire and Wharfe to the wide moors which surround Swaledale and Arkengarthdale and stretch north-west of Tan Hill.

The Great Scar Limestone is responsible for the splendid scenery of Craven. Economically its great value now is as a source of high purity lime for chemical purposes, although the large quarries now working it degrade vast quantities to be used as road metal and aggregates just as has happened with the fine slates. The large quarries in Great Scar Limestone are at Ribble-head, Horton-in-Ribblesdale, Giggleswick, Swinden near Cracoe, Skyrethornes and Kilnsey Crag. The large quarries between Redmire and Leyburn which send limestone to the steel works of Teesside are in Yoredale limestones. The huge quarries opened in the Ingletonian for road stone are at Skirwith near Ingleton; the Silurian is quarried at Dry Rigg, Arco Wood and Helwith Bridge quarries in Ribblesdale. In the past limestone rubble (irregular stones) has been used to a small extent as a building stone but this was mostly gathered from the abundant boulders in the glacial drift. In the older buildings and also in much of the enclosure field walling a pleasing mixture of these boulders with grit boulders and grit flags gives a variety to their texture and colour. Throughs for the walls were quarried in a few special places and were often carried some distance. A secondary but very important use of the limestone has been as a manure for land dressing. For this purpose many scores of lime-kilns have been built of several patterns and these make a prominent feature among Dales buildings. They range from the small single kiln serving one or two farms to the larger "selling" kilns or even double kilns, selling lime to a large surrounding area.

The kiln is a short sturdy tower enclosing the kiln basin within a very solid mass of masonry which is necessary to resist the stresses set up by the changes in temperature. The kiln body has an entry usually on the side facing downhill, in which the bottom of the bowl-shaped kiln is reached. Here there is an ash grate and means of drawing the burned lime. The top of the kiln is open for the tipping in of loads of broken limestone and fuel—usually a coal got from nearby Yoredale strata. The kiln is usually set partly into the hillside below a small quarry which has provided the limestone and often in the northern dales not far from the low quality and cheap coal of which there are many seams under the Yoredale limestones and lower Millstone grits. The lime produced can then be carried downhill to the fields where it was wanted or to the village where some was wanted for builders' mortar.[1]

The Yoredale Series is a group of rocks about a thousand feet in total thickness, made up of shales, sandstones and limestones, sometimes with a coal seam in the sandstone, this little group forming a unit or in modern terminology a "cyclothem". This unit is repeated many times and always in this order, and each is distinguished by the name of its limestone. The thickness of the units varies very widely, as for instance the limestone of the Hardraw Scar and Main units may be as much as 80 or even a hundred feet thick while the limestone of the Three Yard unit is not often more than ten feet. The sandstones are more frequently about 50 feet thick but are usually large lenticles and vary much in quality from one part to another. Of the sandstones, many have been very important building stones and small quarries are to be found near most villages in Yoredale country. These usually provided roughly broken blocks to make "random" walling (see chapter 5 for a description of the different varieties of walling), or in a few places the rock split into flags of thickness from about six inches, which could be broken into very regular building stones, down to an inch or so, to provide roofing slates.

There is evidence that the detritus which forms these rocks was brought into this area by rivers flowing from a continental area then lying to the north and/or the north-west, and that much of this detritus was deposited in a shallow sea. Such deposits would have the form of a delta very much like the present Mississippi delta. They would have extensive sandbanks near the shore passing into muds, first coarse then finer going away from the shore towards deeper water. Eventually when all the detritus was got rid of there would be a clear water sea. The deltaic sands became sandstone during geological time, with an

1. Lime kilns and their operation are fully described in *Old Yorkshire Dales*, A. Raistrick, 1971, chapter 5, Country limekilns, pp. 73-89.

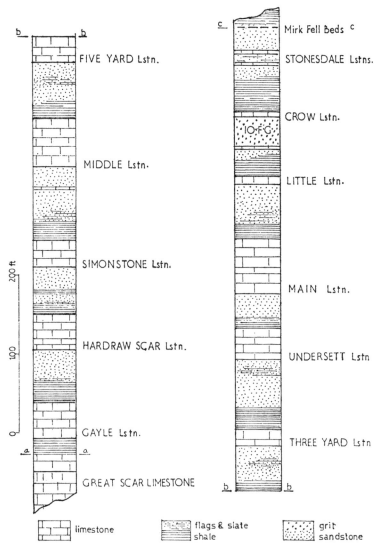

Average section of Yoredale Series in Wensleydale and Swaledale.

increasing intermixture of shale or fine silt. Near the shore they would form coarse, thick sandstones, then progressively fine sandstones, flagstones, sandy shale and slates. In the clear water beyond the shale zone, calcareous organism would flourish, foramanifera, corals, shell fish and some siliceous sponges, and their remains went to make a calcareous mud which has become limestone. We need not here discuss the complex mechanisms of earth movements which are necessary to produce the rhythmic repetition of limestone, shale and sandstone characteristic of the sequence. We must however notice that deposition will be coarsest and thickest towards the source and will become progressively thinner away from it. This is why the Yoredale rocks from north to south vary in coarseness and thickness of individual beds and groups.

In 1835 Phillips chose Wensleydale as his type area and named the series the Yoredales because here there is a fairly good balance of sandstones, limestones and shales. On Alston Moor (South Tyne, Weardale and Teesdale) the same Yoredale Series is present but the limestones are much thinner and the sandstones dominate, coarse and thick and numerous, and the limestones are split into two or three layers by shale partings. In our area the limestones increase in thickness and shales and sandstones become thinner between Swaledale and Wharfedale. The sandstones and flags which are such a feature of the northern dales are very poorly developed or absent in the southern parts. This has been responsible for very noticeable differences in the building stones available in the different dales.

The Yoredale Series will be made clearer by a diagram which might be taken as typical of the Wensleydale development. It is clear in this diagram that there are sandstones fifty or sixty feet thick between the successive limestones and that most of them have flaggy sections in them. In the nineteenth century some quarries in these were expanded into large commercial ventures, some of them employing scores of men and some over a hundred. Much building stone of all kinds was sent into East Lancashire when the railway was completed through Wensleydale to Hawes Junction (Garsdale). The junction line from Hellifield to Burnley made rail transport available right through from Hawes to the expanding textile towns where the building demand was rapidly increasing. It is one of the ironies of changing times that slums created then are now being cleared and roof slates and building stone originally quarried in the Dales are being returned at high prices for new and expensive building often near their place of origin.

The rhythmic form of the Yoredale Series has its effect on the scenery perhaps more noticeably than in the buildings. If we look at the valley near Askrigg, looking to the south side the outstanding shape is that of several terraces or steps made by limestone scars. The long terrace of the Hardraw Scar limestone is that on the edge of which the road runs from Worton to Aysgarth, while above it are other scars made by the Simonstone and Middle limestones. The summit of Addlebrough is a small cap of Undersett limestone. This terraced profile is characteristic of the Yoredales of both Swaledale and Wharfedale as soon as one gets higher up the valley side than the trough, which in these narrower valleys allows only a view of the first limestone scar from the road level.

In looking at the buildings in the different dales differences are most apparent in the size and shape of the stones used in the main walls, in forming the openings for doors and windows and for the roof. These are seen most easily in the smaller houses and the farm buildings as they have most likelihood of being built from the nearest quarry. The builders of the larger houses and mansions may have been able to afford the cost of a better stone brought from a distance, as for instance some of the best stone in Malham Tarn House was brought from Greets quarry above Castle Bolton in Wensleydale. The stone most likely to be the same through a large part of one dale is that used for window sills, lintels and mullions as these need to be strong when cut into the long narrow sections and not many quarries provided stone of suitable quality. Both mason work and transport made these expensive items. In most areas the strong and massive grits of the Millstone Grit have been the source and as this rock is often found only high up on the fells only a few quarries have been opened. In Airedale the quarries on Embsay Fell, Rilstone Fell and Roughaw supplied stone for Skipton Castle and later produced sills, lintels, mullions and roof ridging and sometimes six feet long door jambs for much of the area around. Those who know these quarries well can recognise their products also in much of the eighteenth and early nineteenth century house detail whatever the main walling may be. In Wharfedale huge quarries at Ilkley and Addingham supplied the mid dale and Addingham also quarried millstones which were sent over much of the dales—even as far as Bainbridge mill when it was rebuilt in the eighteenth century. Upper Wharfedale was largely supplied from the quarries of Burnsall and Thorpe Fells where the same Millstone Grit as the Embsay quarries was worked. This stone can be seen in the Fountains Hospital at Linton, and in later copings and massive parapets on some of the county bridges. The most striking perhaps is in the little road bridge at the bottom of Threshfield village where individual stones can be seen up to ten feet long, two feet square section and weighing something near two and a half tons.

In Nidderdale the Scott Gate Ash quarries near Pateley Bridge were for a long time famous and, though most of their stone was sent away to the cities and for export, it was used widely in local building of the nineteenth century. As the whole of the upper dale is Millstone Grit, which everywhere has provided good building stone, there is more uniformity in the buildings of that dale than in the others. Some of the finest use of this stone is to be seen in the impressive masonry dams of the Bradford reservoirs at Angram and Scar House. These are the same rock as Skipton Castle and Linton Hospital.

In Wensleydale and Swaledale there is a fine grit in strata that used to be classed as the upper part of the Yoredales but is now by some classed as the basal beds of the Millstone Grit. Among this group is the so called Ten Fathom Grit, 60 feet being its usual thickness. It is very hard and fine grained, often occurs in six or eight inch flags and these can be cut cleanly into very regular sized building stones. In the head of Swaledale around Muker and Keld it is well developed and not very high above the valley level. There are many small quarries in it near to the villages and most of the buildings are made with it, the roofs being covered with slates of high quality brought from the Hill Top quarries not far away in Birkdale. The houses and farm buildings in Angram offer splendid examples of this building stone and are very striking for the regularity of the coursing of the stone. There is another good grit above the Crow limestone above the Ten Fathom Grit but below the Tan Hill Coal which has been used widely. The Ten Fathom Grit is also developed and quarried in the upper parts of Arkengarthdale.

Penhill summit and the fell tops between successive dales provide Millstone Grit. The geological structure however is such that massive beds such as the Grassington Grits come in to the south but are missing in the dales to the north. On Penhill some lower Millstone Grit beds are present, including the famous slate and flag beds which have covered roofs in much of the Dales housing and were worked at several quarries around Carlton and above West Witton. These are the same approximately as the fine flags of Hill Top quarry.

In the western dales of Ribblesdale, Dentdale and Garsdale great differences in the style and details of buildings will be obvious if they are looked for. These valleys have no easily access-ible Millstone Grit except on Baugh Fell north of Garsdale, where there are a few good quarries on the west side overlooking the Rawthey valley. The bottom of Dentdale is occupied by the Great Scar Limestone, and then the succeeding Yoredale Lime-stones are thin, but the fine series of flags and slates above the Middle Limestone have been extensively quarried at the head of Deepdale, the southern tributary of the Dee, in the High Pike quarries. The flags and slates under the Middle limestone have been quarried in Scotcher Gill just north of Dent.[2] The building in Dentdale is made characteristic by the use of abundant cut flag and the slates from Scotcher Gill. The absence of Millstone Grit has caused flags, sometimes two or three on top of one another, to be used for window lintels in many small buildings. The sides of windows and doors are often made as walls carefully built, in the absence of large jambs. For better houses stone has been brought from West Baugh Fell. There are a few small quarries, mostly underground levels, on the south side of Garsdale along Risehill side: these have been for flags, but must not be confused with a few coal levels. There is also a quarry at Bridge End in the flags above the Three Yard Limestone. The largest quarry, however, in this north-western corner of the Dales is Rawthey Quarry in Uldale, the upper valley of the Rawthey. This is on the river side, two miles above Rawthey Bridge and in the sandstones between the Middle and Five Yard Limestone. This quarry with those on Baugh Fell provided much of the stone for the town of Sedbergh.

In Ribblesdale the Studfold Sandstone and some of the Horton Flags have been widely used and houses of these materials are very different in appearance from those of flaggy sandstone. There is much irregularity in the splitting of the stones and great skill has been exercised in their use. In many buildings a limestone rubble in random coursing has been used, with good quoins and throughs of Horton Flag holding them.

We must not ignore the limestones because they have occasionally been used to great effect. The finest structures both as buildings and as architecture are the railway viaducts in Dentdale. The Dent Head, one of the finest, is based upon the Hardraw Scar Limestone but built from the Simonstone Limestone quarried just up the gill. Arten Gill viaduct is also of limestone. Some of the parapets were made of Penrith (Permian) sandstone, brought from the Vale of Eden. The limestones of Dentdale are better known for their exploitation as Dent Marble. The Simonstone is often very compact and a good uniform black colour. There are very many small quarries all round Dentdale and Garsdale in this limestone which was carried to Stone House in Dentdale to be sawn and polished. A whiter limestone was more valued and a grey, the commonest, richly ornamented with sections of fossil crinoids, was used for heavier work, particularly the fireplaces and kerbs of railway stations. Much of the finer black and white was cut into flooring tiles—these can be seen in Dent and many other churches—and a great export trade, particularly to Australia, developed in these. There were at one time shipping offices and agents in Newcastle, Liverpool and London. In all the

2. These quarries extend for half a mile along the face of Kirk Bank.

dales limestone rubble from the glacial rubbish has been used for walling, helped by gritstone or slate throughs and tops, and the number of little walling quarries near rubble walls is many scores, possibly even hundreds.

A further comment is needed for Settle and Ingleton. The Craven Fault has along that line brought down the Millstone Grit on the south side making it available, so that, although the scenery (all to the north) is that of limestone of spectacular quality, the towns are essentially Millstone Grit, and enjoy doorways with fine moulded headstones and buildings with such complex windows as those of the Folly at Settle. The only comparable building in the northern dales is, or rather was, Askrigg Old Hall. Its windows closely resembled those of the Folly.

In summary one can say that this mid-Pennine area is perhaps the very best example of the upland "stone belt" of many architectural writers. Building stones are found in all parts in a variety sufficient to meet every requirement of the builder. Also the variety is distributed from place to place in such a way as to ensure that each dale has a character of its own to which the underlying geology has contributed not only to the topography and scenery, but also to the appearance of the buildings through the materials most readily available.

2.   The Early Period of Building

DOMESTIC building began when groups of prehistoric people exchanged a nomadic way of life for one which was based upon agriculture rather than on hunting. Sowing seed and waiting for the harvest tied a family to one location and this created a need for a permanent home more substantial than the skin tent of the nomad. Huts provided a shelter from the weather, a place in which to sleep even when cooking, eating and working were still done out in the open. Shelter for stock and stores was also required and this was found in the small enclosures around the hut. The earliest huts we can recognise in our area belong to the Bronze Age of something like three milleniums ago and are seen now as circular walls of rough stone which were the foundations for a hut built of light timber and thatch. During the Iron Age the hut diameters were generally smaller and a low side wall of timber sometimes stood on the stone foundation and lifted the roof to a comfortable height. It was the Roman example which led the Romano-British Brigantes to make the exceptional rectangular huts, but remains of ‹ types are still limited to foundations and occasional post-holes.

The Roman invaders in the first centuries AD were the first to build houses, granaries and forts in proper mason-built fashion, but little of these true buildings has survived except foundations and only a few of these are now uncovered. The fort at Bainbridge and the town at Aldborough are the best of these. After the withdrawal of the Romans very little stone building was done through the Dark Ages except in connection with the church. A small stone house on Malham Moor, the so-called Priest's house at SD 897674, is a small building 15 ft. by 9 ft. inside with two slender partition walls. The outside walls are made with a double row of boulders up to one 6 ft. long by 4 ft. wide set on edge, the spaces between the rows being carefully packed with smaller boulders. Above these the building was ot timber. More skilful mason building is to be seen in the crypt of Ripon Cathedral built about 670 AD, but for the rest the huts of the general population were no more than roughly made timber hovels and it is doubtful if even their foundations could be recognised.

It is not until the Anglian invasions of the seventh and eighth centuries that houses of a regular structural pattern began to be built. These were still limited to the houses of the more important people and the greater part of the folk still made what hovels they could contrive out of light timber or perhaps of sods and clay blocks. The new form of building with "crucks" however was important as it remained a principal form for many centuries, used for houses, barns and probably for the first churches.*

It was in the late sixth century that the Angles founded the kingdom of Northumbria and in the early seventh century began the movement into the lower part of the Dales which open from the Vale of York. It was these people who cleared woodland along the river side and made the settlements which became so many of our present villages. They were followed in the eighth century by Danish invaders who settled more villages, to some of which they gave their own names like Thoralby—Thorold's farm. Most villages were made by a small group of families with a head man whose house was sometimes larger than most of the huts and built on a new structural plan. In a few villages, churches were built but Bede says, "In those days the English people were accustomed to gather together wherever a priest came to their village, at his call, to hear the Word." Only in a few places the thegn or overlord might build a small wooden church and this with a graveyard became the centre of a parish of great extent. Such early churches were built at Wensley and Kirkby Malham, and probably at Grinton, Burnsall and other places where the ecclesiastical parish includes a large number of townships like Aysgarth and Grinton.

At some churches, and preaching places which later became churches, wooden staves and crosses were set up which in some cases were soon replaced in stone. These were carved with elaborate patterns, the work of a small group of masons, and they are our oldest elaborate mason work in the Dales. Fragments of these crosses are to be seen in several churches, Easby, Wensley, Burnsall and Gargrave having several in each. The Norse invaders, who came to the Pennines by way of the route round Scotland to the north of Ireland and the Isle of Man and then to the Lancashire and Lake District coast, spread over the higher fells where the Anglo-Danish had not settled. They were sheep farmers and lived in isolated farms and not in villages. They brought some culture with them, and many of the later crosses include in their carving motifs which are of Norse origin.

The earliest large buildings in stone are the castles, monasteries

---

* This form of house building will be discussed in a later chapter.

and churches, and the earliest of these are of the twelfth century by which time the Normans had settled themselves in control of the country. The years after the Conquest were occupied in the settlement and control of the native population and the Normans' task was to build fortresses as quickly as possible in strategic places. For speed these were built of earthwork and timber, with enforced labour, and were in the form of "motte and bailey". There is a splendid example at Middleham known as William's Hill. This is just south of the castle within a field's length. It was built by Ribald, the brother of Red Conan of Richmond, and is a circular motte, 40 ft. high surrounded by a 20 ft. ditch with an outer bank 9 ft. high. On the summit of the mound there is an area 160 ft. by 115 ft. where there is a platform on which a wooden tower stood; there is also a small sunk court 85 ft. by 55 ft. in which a timber hall stood. The bailey is a large enclosure at one side of the motte surrounded by a ditch with a 13 ft. high rampart on the inside, within which were crowded domestic and garrison buildings. This was all abandoned about 1190 when the stone castle was built. There is another interesting motte and bailey at Sedbergh where the top of a natural hill of rock has been cut and scarped to make the motte. No trace of building now remains but its position and shape make it a prominent feature on the edge of the town as seen from the Kirkby Stephen road.

The timber castles were made in a great hurry; the large motte at York known as Baile Hill was built in only eight days and until the mid-twelfth century this was the only kind of castle. In 1154 Richmond Castle was one of the first to have stonework. The site was so strong that the bailey was made with only a ramp on the edge of the cliff overlooking the river, and stone walls on the north-east and north-west making a triangular area which in other circumstances would have had a motte at the apex. Part of this old bailey wall on the north-east is now exposed with its typical Norman herringbone pattern walling. In the change from timber to stone building, the motte tower became the "keep" and the bailey ditch was replaced by the curtain wall. In Richmond Castle we have one of the finest early castles in the country. The great scale of the keep of 1160 is outstanding among contemporary military architecture, equalled only by London and Rochester. It is 100 ft. 6 ins. high and of rectangular plan 55 ft. by 45 ft. The plain walls are broken up by vertical narrow buttresses from ground to battlements. The old gate-house entry was blocked at some time and an entry made at first floor level. A central pillar supports the first floor and another makes a central support for the beams of the second floor. This pattern of Richmond keep was followed at Appleby, Brough and Brougham within the next few years.

In the south-east corner of the great court or bailey, Scolland's Hall—named after a servant of the first Earl Allan and built soon after the keep—is one of the earliest domestic buildings of its kind in the country. It was the dwelling place of the Earl, the keep being entirely for military and not domestic use. The hall is of two storeys, the ground floor being cellars and store-rooms. An outside stair reaches the finely moulded doorway to the first floor. The hall has a solar or private living room at the east end and two round-headed two-light windows give light. Some alterations were made later at the west end to give access to a buttery and kitchen. This is one of our oldest Dales' domestic buildings.*

The stone for the castle was got not far away on Aske Moor and Richmond Out Moor, from several quarries in the grits below the Undersett Limestone. The building was done by masons and carpenters brought over from Normandy, directed by a master mason. It is not known if they had plans drawn by an architect for them to work to, but judging by the similarities in the keeps of other castles of the same period it seems more likely that the master masons worked to a common pattern which they knew from their training and experience. The general form was a translation of the timber tower and hall of the earthwork motte into the keep and hall now built of stone and in a larger and permanent form. The massive stone keep could only have been built on a solid foundation for which an earthern motte would have been quite useless—only solid rock could carry the great weight of these new structures. The shape of the castle site made the ditches of the bailey unnecessary and the bank of the bailey became the stone curtain wall. In fact William's Hill is almost an earth and timber prototype for Richmond Castle.

In some details, particularly the plain walling, the Norman work was often crude or clumsy with wide joints and a poor mortar. By the end of the twelfth century the workmanship had improved and this can be seen in the finer mouldings of the doorway and windows of Scolland's Hall. Nonetheless the walls and some of the buildings were repaired from time to time, and in 1485 when the abandonment of the castle was being discussed a survey of its condition was made and the repairs required to be done make a formidable list. The keep, though the oldest building, required least repair but the walls of the bailey and other buildings required repairs and replacements which add up to the following total. There were 1,127 yards of wall to repair or rebuild, ten corbels and sixteen spouts (gargoyles) to replace and 24 lengths of crest (battlements). Replacement of decayed timber needed 630 oak trees, the roofs would take 42 tons of sheet lead

* An excellent guide book is on sale at the castle and should be used for further detail.

and a ton of iron was wanted for the gate and other matters. The pieces of crest were the very large stones which made the battlement of the keep. Many castles were almost past repair by the fifteenth century and were allowed to fall to ruin. Some were cleared entirely and completely rebuilt, as was Skipton.

Middleham Castle, though built only twenty years or so later, was of a very different type. The keep was much larger in area than that of Richmond and is closely surrounded by other buildings across a surrounding space little more than an alleyway. The outer walls of these buildings form the greater part of the curtain wall. This different plan may in part be due to masons with a different tradition and experience, or because the castle was designed more as being a strong defensive post and at the same time a fortified residence of importance. Skipton Castle was probably built as a motte and bailey as the outer wall of the grounds still flanks one side of the road and an area called The Bailey. It was however almost entirely rebuilt and extended to a baronial mansion by Lady Anne Clifford.

At Skipton the stone for the rebuilding and for extensions was the same as in the earlier work and the quarries are named and known. It came from the Millstone Grit of Embsay Crag, Embsay Moor (Stoney Rigg quarries), Rilston Fell (Fairy Chest) and Roughaw. The quarries remained in use, with their sled roads, until the late seventeenth century when they were supplying lintels, sills, mullions and roof rigging for the general house building in the area, and some were making millstones. The master masons at Skipton who were building a tower in 1437 were Robert and Thomas Hawmond who worked for 46 weeks and had 18d. each, without food, each week. Among other items of expense were the hire of a crane from Bolton Priory, its carriage from Bolton, and then the cost of raising stone with it to the top of the tower. Getting stone at Staynrig quarry, 112 loads, cost 6d. a load; labourers getting the stone to the top of the tower as building proceeded during 110 days, and carrying clay and sand, got 4d. a day; they also brought lime from the Prior of Bolton and some from Addingham. A master mason, Bellerby, was brought in to make the battlements and special free stone was got for this. Many of the men were brought in from other places as the Vicar of Skipton had 33s. 10d. for their board. Old lead was melted and used to roof the tower.

Bolton Castle in Wensleydale is a fourteenth century structure but much information on the process of its building is available. Sir Richard Scrope about 1370 was granted a licence to crenellate his manor house, that is to fortify it with walls and battlements, and he used this as an excuse to replace the old house by a castle. This he began to build on the west side of his manor house and, this part being completed, he pulled down his old house and lived in the new, the west and part of the south wings, while the rest of the castle was built. The stone for the castle was got in local quarries, those for the walling being on Bolton Parks just behind the village. It is the flaggy sandstone which occurs between the Five Yard Limestone and the Undersett Limestone and its use creates an unusual impression on first sight. As the castle is approached by the steep road which comes up by the south-east corner, any careful observer will be struck by the smallness and thinness of the walling stones which seem incongruous and all out of proportion for such a massive building. The quoins, window and door framing and parapets, as well as fireplaces, stairs and other internal detail, are of much larger stone from the Greets Quarry about three miles away. This is the Ten Fathom Grit of the Upper Yoredale Series.

John Lewyn was the master mason with whom the contract for building the east and north wings was made. He was a man already of great experience who had been in charge of building at Carlisle, Roxburgh and Dunstanburgh castles and no doubt had built the earlier part of Bolton. He was mason to the Bishop of Durham about 1370 and had been employed by the king to repair Bamburgh Castle in 1368. The contract for Bolton Castle was made with Lewyn in 1378 and specifies the sizes of the many rooms and of the north-east and south-east towers and the gatehouse. Outer walls were to be seven and a half feet thick and inner walls four feet. Lewyn was to get all the stone and lime but Sir Richard would provide carriage for these, wood as fuel for the limekiln which Lewyn would build for making lime for his mortar, and also timber for all his scaffolding. From Leland we learn that the building of the whole castle took eighteen years and the total cost was 1,000 marks (about £650). Long enough timber could not be got in the Dales so long logs were brought from Inglewood Forest in the Vale of Eden and were carried in waggons by stages, drawn from place to place by teams of oxen.

Half the castle is still intact; the north-east tower fell in 1761 and most of the building except the west wing was deroofed and stripped of its wooden floors in the general slighting of 1655. The castle is built around a courtyard with only one entrance through a very strong gatehouse in the south-east corner. From the courtyard five narrow doorways defended by portcullis, all alike, led by tortuous stairs and passages to different parts of the castle. If an enemy penetrated the yard and entered by any of these doors there was still no dirct way from one part of the building to another. Any journey about the castle involves many stairs up and down, between passages which seem to have no plan and no regular direction, leading to unexpected rooms which have to be crossed for the continuation. The inside of the castle, except for those who have spent a long time "learning" it, can be very much of a puzzle maze. The rooms of the gatehouse and south-east tower were for the garrison, but the rest are commodious and domestic, with generous windows and fireplaces. The hall in the north wing, 51 ft. by 27 ft. and two storeys in height, was nearly matched by a "great chamber" 47 ft. long and 25 ft. wide in the west wing. Everywhere there is evidence of spacious comfort. Throughout it is clear that the castle was first a baronial mansion upon which enormous ingenuity has been expended in giving it strength and security if put to the siege. As Lewyn undertook many other jobs during the time the castle at Bolton was being built, it is clear that the work on the site was left in the capable hands of master masons with Lewyn visiting from time to time to check and advise. This may have been the way many of the master builders of the time operated, much as architects do now.

The other castle building in the Dales area is confined to Bowes, Ripley, Knaresborough and Skipton with two smaller ones on the western side, Pendragon and Lammerside. Bowes Castle stands in the mouth of Stainmore on the eastern side and is peculiar in being an isolated keep with no bailey or other buildings. It was built in the twelfth century by Count Alan of Normandy as one of his several points of defence against and supervision of the conquered natives. It is a massive square tower with buttressed walls over twelve feet thick, some parts of which are still fifty feet high. The entrance was in the east side and at the first floor, and by a stairway under a covered structure. There is yet some evidence of a moat which surrounded it but no trace of any other building or accommodation. It is built within the Roman fort of Lavatrae from which its stone was taken. The internal arrangements can still be deduced—the ground floor with vaulted roof was divided into three rooms and the first floor into two. It was in this first floor that the governor or commander would have his living rooms. There are some small chambers in the thickness of the walls. A third floor was evidently for the small garrison which occupied it as a watch tower to protect the Stainmore Pass, a regular route for invaders coming from the north-west and Scotland. The Scots attacked and damaged the castle in 1173 and more seriously in the fourteenth century. It was then reduced to such a condition as to need extensive repair and partial rebuilding.

On the other side of the Pennines in the mouth of Mallerstang is Pendragon Castle, like Bowes only a rectangular keep. It mainly differs in being almost entirely rebuilt by Lady Anne Clifford in the seventeenth century. It is more related to the larger pele towers of the northern counties and the Borders than to the more regular Norman castles. The site was first occupied by a timber tower towards the end of the twelfth century and about 1300 passed into the possession of Robert Clifford who strengthened it. In a Scots raid in 1341 it was burned down but Roger Clifford restored it, building in stone, between 1360 and 1370. Leland saw it in 1539 but it was again attacked and burned by the Scots in 1541. After this very troublous history it remained as a ruin for more than a century until Lady Anne Clifford included it in 1660 in her extensive programme of castle restoration. It was "dismantled" in 1685 so had an unusually short life. It is now a ruin but Mr. Raven Frankland has done much to clear away the debris and reveal sufficient to show clearly what was its structure. It is a stone tower 64 feet square with slight corner buttresses, the walls about 11 feet thick. It was formerly three storeys high. There are mounds and part of a ditch which are the remains of an enclosing wall and buildings of a defence added by Lady Anne. A peculiar feature shared with Bowes is the presence in the thickness of the walls of barrel-vaulted L-shaped chambers in the north-east and south-west corners of the ground floor and all the four corners of the first floor. The few windows are round-headed of one or two lights.

Coming back to the east side of the Pennines, only one other castle needs mention here, because it is a very important link between the early defensive castles and the later group of fortified houses. It is Ripley Castle south of Ripon and in the valley of the Nidd. This in part is a very early tower house of the twelfth century, square and massive. It was strengthened at a later date and then enlarged and partly rebuilt in 1555. An early manor house adjoined this tower which as late as 1773 was described by Pennant: — "A more ancient house still remains of wood and plaster and wooden stairs. The entrance to the house is through a porch ... the hall is large and lofty, has bow windows, its elevated upper table and its table for vassals, and is floored with brick." This is the description which we shall meet again in the smaller halls. Very soon after this it was pulled down and new sections were built. Now only the gatehouse, the great tower and a part of the south range are old.

So far we have seen two transformations from timber to stone structures, one in the later years of the twelfth century when timber tower castles were abandoned for new ones of stone, as at Middleham and Pendragon, and the start of a later change from mid-sixteenth century to about the beginning of the eighteenth, when first manor houses, then larger yeomen's houses, and finally peasants' and artisans' hovels and hutments gave place to small stone cottages. These changes we shall describe in later chapters in some detail.

3.

Monasteries, Churches and Bridges

AFTER the castles the best known of the larger buildings are the monasteries in the lower dales. Egglestone, Easby, Jervaulx, Coverham, Fountains and Bolton make a wonderful architectural and historic heritage. They have been adequately described over and over again and excellent guide books and much more extensive works are available to help the visitor to appreciate them. This book will say little about them, except to attempt in a brief manner the answer to the question which is so often asked: "Who built them, and how?" The popular answer, "The monks", is not acceptable so the question is still there. To give an answer with some basis in fact we must know a little about the organisation of the communities of monks and the workers who built churches, bridges, castles and monasteries.

Although there were several different orders of monks, for instance Cistercians at Fountains, Premonstratensians at Easby, Augustinians at Bolton, Benedictines at St. Martin's, all the monks known as "religious" had taken vows to devote their time to prayer and meditation, with only a few of them serving as officials looking after the affairs of the community. Besides the monks there was a number of "lay brethren" who were attached to and a part of the community, with their own quarters in the monastery, but who had not taken religious vows. They worked with their hands—servants in the kitchen, workers on the fields or at the granges, and craftsmen, masons, carpenters and so on. It was the lay brethren with other workers who made and maintained the buildings and who provided the necessaries for the life of the monks. There was another group, the "oblates", who did not live in the monastery but were men hired for wages to do unskilled labouring, carrying and other work. A large monastery might have a few score lay brethren and a comparable number of oblates. Whitaker said that Bolton Priory with only 20 canons had nearly 200 lay brethren, but this number must have included all the people who worked on the priory farms as well as the lay brethren.

The general practice when building or extending a monastery was to employ a master mason who in some ways resembled the present day architect. He could design or knew designs of buildings and could organise labour and the supply of materials. He might be one of the lay brethren or, more often, was hired for the particular job for which he might make a contract. Among remaining accounts the Fabric Rolls of York Minster make all this building organisation clear and can be used as a general indication for what was done at most of the monasteries.

In addition to the available lay brethren the master mason would hire a number of masons, master masons, rough masons and apprentices, quarrymen, labourers and sometimes plasterers. There was also a master carpenter who, together with a staff of lay brethren and oblates, would include woodmen, sawyers, joiners, carvers and labourers. Some monasteries like York Minster owned their own quarries but if not, then the master mason would have to find and lease one. The more skilled of the masons were the hewers who could select and win stone in the quarry, rough shape it there and finish it or even carve it on the site. A second group of the masons was the setters or layers who did the actual stone laying and building with stone prepared for them by the masons. The stone at the quarry was scapelled, that is rough dressed with axes, hammers and picks (called stone-axes and stone-picks), and then was fine dressed and shaped at York, and the same procedure was carried out at all the monasteries. The builders in the dales were able to find good stone near at hand and transport was little more than a short sled journey.

Masons and apprentices lived in a "lodge" which was a temporary timber building at the site; it usually included several rooms in some of which the finer stone cutting and carving was done. In another room the wooden patterns to which mouldings were made were stored, and special details could be drawn out on thin board. Some of the larger elements, like the pattern of a window for making its tracery and arch, could be drawn out full size on a large floor, either whole or in parts. Some mouldings like string courses which were almost standard and wanted in vast quantity, sometimes hundreds of feet of the same pattern, were excellent training for apprentices and were largely their work. The master mason was in charge of all the building and was master of the lodge, responsible for discipline, for hiring labour, and for seeing that the quality of building and materials was maintained. He received pay usually as an agreed sum, yearly or on completion, and a gown yearly.

The carpenters did not usually have a comparable "lodge" organisation except that they worked under their master carpenter and were sometimes family groups. The master carpenters could do fine carving and could design and make elaborate roofs and screens. The woodmen, besides felling trees selected by the master carpenter, would help the sawyers to cut them up to the direction of the master and to his measurement and marking out. Joints would be cut at the sheds on the site and much of this was done by those who became called "joiners". Trusses for the roof were made and assembled on the ground, checked and all joints marked before the truss was erected to position. These joiners' marks can be seen in many church roofs. We have seen in discussing Bolton Castle that the master mason Lewyn had worked at several castles and for the Bishop of Durham, and most master masons had comparable varied experience on many buildings. This is how patterns and styles were spread, so that some details—forming of doorways with their mouldings, string courses and some other features—are of the same or very similar pattern in more than one building.

The plan of the monastery was set by each different Order but the basis was the same in all of them. The large church formed one side of a cloister area, on the other sides of which were usually a chapter house and other rooms, on the side opposite the church the kitchens and refectory, and on the fourth side the quarters of the lay brethren. There were individual variants of this general plan but it would be perfectly familiar to the builders.

Besides working at the monasteries the master masons travelled about to take other contracts, churches and bridges, palaces, castles and large houses. The King's buildings were made and maintained by conscript masons and labourers so that some had a wide experience on more than one kind of building. The conscripts were gathered on royal warrant by the Sheriffs of the counties, and some were taken for three years.

The monasteries and churches contained much finely carved woodwork besides the roof, in screens, stalls and benches, pulpit and lectern and other furnishings. This carving was done by teams of carpenters who travelled from one contract to another, much as the masons did. We are fortunate in the Dales in having much of the work of these teams still to be seen, preserved for us in churches to which it was removed at the Dissolution. William Bromflet, sometimes called William Carver, with some of his family and a small team were all members of the Joiners' Guild of Ripon and, working together, had developed a style and used details of their own by which their work can be recognised. About 1527 they carved very elaborate screens for the Scrope chantry in Easby Abbey and, at the Dissolution, John Lord Scrope claimed these and removed them to Wensley church where they are now to be seen as the Bolton parclose or pew. The stalls from Easby Abbey, with their interesting miserere carvings under the seats and the splendid canopies, were removed to Richmond Parish Church where they are used as the stalls for the Corporation, choir and officiating clergy. About the same time this team made the splendid screen and some pews for Jervaulx Abbey and these are now preserved in Aysgarth church, the screen entire, and two carved bench ends used to make the reading desk. The screen was originally painted and sufficient traces of the colours remained for the whole to be restored. The earliest work we have of theirs is at Ripon Minster where the choir stalls, with canopies and misereres, and the screen were made by them in the years 1489 to 1494. Some accounts and contracts for their work in the Minster survive for the year 1518. Some other work of this team can be seen at Manchester, 1506; Bridlington Priory, 1519; and Beverley, 1520 to 1524. Other teams of carpenters and masons whose names have not been kept were moving about the country taking contracts for work in monasteries, churches and halls.

One of the early masons' contracts was for Catterick Church in 1412. There was an old church there at the time, but in 1412 Dame Katherine, widow of John de Burgh, with her son William decided to build a new church. For this they made a contract with a mason, Richard of Crakehall, who agreed to take "full charge for to make the Kirke of Katrick newe als Werkemanschippe and mason crafte will". He would find all necessary labour and for materials he could pull down the old church and use the stone after the timber was taken out. The timber was kept for the carpenter who would be making the roof, screens and furnishings. The mason dug the foundations on the new site and carried the stone from the old church. All extra stone was to be got at his own cost at a quarry which he would hire, but Katherine and William de Burgh would provide all carriage from the quarry and also all lime, and the scaffolding and centres for arches, but these were to remain their property when the job was complete. The main body of the contract specified the overall dimensions of the church, thickness and height of walls and their pattern with battlements, where windows were to be placed (a window from the old church could be used for one), the number of pillars in the nave and their height, the mason being left to work within these general guide lines. He was left to make the work and ornament as he thought right. On completion within three years he was to receive 170 marks, that is about £114, and a gown. The mason's wage was then 7d. a day, a carpenter 5d. and a quarryman 3¾d.

In a contract in 1409 for building a south aisle onto Hornby church in Wensleydale, Conyers of Hornby said it must have an arcade of two pillars and two responds, four windows and three buttresses. The roof was to be covered with lead and glass and ironwork provided in two windows. The time taken was to be eight months and the pay £40. The mason was left with these bare instructions, leaving it to his skill and experience to match walls, windows and other details.

During the monastic period, to build a bridge was regarded as an act of piety and, besides church building, masons were employed, usually making stone bridges to replace older timber ones. As late as 1602 the timber bridges at Linton (now called Grassington Bridge) and Burnsall were in ruin and they were rebuilt in stone, Linton in 1603 at public cost, and Burnsall in 1609 at the cost of Sir William Craven. The contract for Catterick Bridge in 1421 gives a lot of information about how the masons worked. Seven local gentry made the contract with three master masons, Thomas Ampleforthe, John Garrett and Robert Maunsell "to make a brigg of stane oure ye water of Swale atte Catrik betwixt ye olde stane brigg and ye New brigge of tre" (timber). It was to be "sufficient and workmanly in Masoncrafte accordand in substance to Barnacastell brigge . . .". The promoters told the masons what they desired and gave them a pattern to show what they wanted.

According to the contract the bridge was to have three arches with two piers and abutments. The employers took a large share of the work—they were to make the coffer dams for building the bridge ends and for the piers when wanted, and to supply centring for the arches. Such scaffolding as was required was to be supplied by them. The masons were to work two quarries, one at Sedbery and one at Rysedale where they got and scapelled (rough shaped) all the stone needed, and then the promoters carried it to the bridge ends. The masons built a lime kiln to make their mortar, provided wood and coal for fuel and found and got all the sand and limestone needed for the mortar. The employers were to build a lodge of timber in which the masons could live and work, and also provided iron and steel for tools. The work was to be completed in three and a half years and the payment was 260 marks and a gown to each mason each year.

All the above conditions and the sharing of work, particularly the carriage and the provision of a lodge for the masons, are common to many of the contracts of the fifteenth and sixteenth centuries. Groups of craftsmen who had worked together in these lodges would sometimes move round the country as a team, perhaps working on a bridge as at Marske. In 1530 in response to the increasing traffic on the roads the Act of Henry VIII, 22, chap. 5, empowered the Justices of the Peace to enquire "of all manner of annoyances of bridges broken in the highways to the damage of the King's liege people", and to estimate the cost of repair or replacement. This cost could be levied on the appropriate district. On the side of the abutment of Burnsall Bridge, for instance, there is a well carved stone with this inscription: THIS BRIDGE WAS REPAIRED AT THE CHARGE OF THE WEST RIDING 1674.

These inscriptions are common on bridges both large and small, such for instance as Barden, Ling Gill and Cowgill in Dentdale. The Justices could also appoint surveyors to examine and oversee the work. Proceedings under the Act were taken at Quarter Sessions but were very slow to begin in the North, and it was not until late in the sixteenth or early seventeenth century that many bridges were built.

In the first fifty years of the seventeenth century nearly all the Dales bridges were repaired or rebuilt in stone on the site of earlier bridges of timber. Time after time the lack of timber suitable, long and large enough for use is noted and the order made for a "new brigg of stone". The seventeenth century work and some that is earlier is to be seen in most of the bridges if it is looked for underneath; the old narrow arch is often incorporated in the present wider bridge and the older ones are usually built on ribs. The newer arch is often flatter than the old one. On the older portions it is common to find mason marks, principally on the piers and on the finer tooled soffit stones of the arches. On a single bridge there is often a moderate variety, ten or a dozen different marks being found. These marks identify the work of different masons who did the stone dressing and shaping and enabled the master mason to keep a check on the work of his men and the quarry banker hands. From the number of marks on the larger bridges it appears that there may have been as many as twelve or even fifteen masons at work. In a few cases similar marks can be recognised on different bridges in one area and this may mean that the same men had worked at these jobs.

Year by year the surveyors reported on and repaired the older bridges, and these reports contain some startling reminders of the changes that have taken place in our main lines of traffic. The bridge at Hubberholme, Wharfedale, is noted as "beinge the high roadeway leading between the markett towne of Lancaster in the countie of Lancaster, and the markett towne of Newcastle-upon-Tyne in the countie of Northumberland". The road thus indicated would be a fairly direct line, Clapham-Helwith Bridge (repaired 1611)-Greenfield-Hubberholme and then Wensley-Richmond-Durham. The bridge was repaired at the cost of the Wapentake in 1639. In 1659 it was said it "not beinge knowne who ought to repaire itt, ordered a greate summe upon ye W.R. beinge £300". It was destroyed soon after in the floods of 1673 and again rebuilt at the cost of the West Riding.

The sixteenth century was a time when many landowners began to replace their timber halls by more elaborate stone buildings, helped in this by the increasing numbers of masons with skill and experience, but the fifteenth and sixteenth centuries in the North were still troubled by the Border wars and by

31

the raiding across the Border. For protection against these troubles the defensive pele towers had been built in large numbers in the northern counties of Cumberland and Northumberland, Westmorland and Durham. The pele is essentially a substantial square stone tower of three storeys, with walls of great thickness and sometimes battlemented. The ground floor compartment may be roofed with a stone vault and generally used for stores or sometimes as a stable or byre. The living quarters were in the first and second floors. The peles date mainly from the late fourteenth century when, after devastation by the Scots before the battle of Neville's Cross in 1374, very many licences to crenelate buildings (make them defensible) were issued. Pele towers were built in nearly every village near the Border. North Yorkshire is almost their southern limit and, in the few we have, the domestic use is more prominent than the military. Pendragon Castle has been described in chapter 2 and is about the best example of a military pele.

The plan and style of the pele passes into the domestic tower-house, like Mortham Tower and Nappa Hall, and is found as part of such halls as Walburn in Swaledale and Markenfield near Ripon. The change is made by adding a large hall to one side of the pele and then a cross wing at the other end of the hall, making a large house in many ways allied to the Elizabethan H-house of the country further south. Some of the peles and tower houses have been absorbed into larger mansions in which they remain as a minor feature. In Aske Hall, near Richmond, the old tower house remains but is almost overshadowed by the extensive later mansion of the Earls of Zetland. Similar absorption has happened at Hornby Castle in Wensleydale and even more completely at Danby.

Related in some ways to these large halls there are in the Dales a few very fine sixteenth and later century houses, each deserving a separate description of their architectural merit and interest, but they do not properly come within the scope of this account of Dales building. Each has been the undertaking of a wealthy individual or family who could employ skilled architects and masons who built in a fashion which could in no sense be called native to the Dales. Among such buildings are the larger halls like Fountains Hall and on a smaller scale but related to it, Friars Head at Winterburn, both remaining very much as they were built. Swinsty Hall in the Washburn, Castle Court at Ilkley and other hall houses more related to the building styles further south are not discussed in this book.

CRUCKED BARN
AT
DREBLEY

RIDGE TREE

COLLAR

PURLIN

SPARS

CRUCK

GABLE WALL

SIDE WALL

Crucked barn at Drebley, between Bolton Abbey and Burnsall, showing part of one cruck with purlins, wind braces, collar and spars. Some of the heather thatch still remains under a corrugated iron roof. This is part of a four-bay building. (Photo: J. Starkie, Yorkshire Dales National Park Committee.)

Thatched barn near Hurst, Swaledale. (Photo: R. B. Fawcett.)

A 19th century field barn in traditional style at Crackpot, Swaledale. Local stone, coping and kneelers and well-cut quoins.

Medieval house — Botton House, Grassington. It was described in 1605 as an ancient "mansion house" belonging to the Earl of Cumberland, and was sold to the Freeholders of Grassington. (Photo: C. Crossthwaite.)

Remains of a 16th century thatched farm at Harkerside, Swaledale.

Cottage of c. 1600 at Grimwith in Appletreewick township, Wharfedale. The upstairs windows were enlarged in the 18th century. Note the very strong quoins and the squared Millstone Grit wallstones well coursed.

House offshut and small farm building, 18th century, all built with Cotterdale flag. The far building shows the line of a former thatched roof.

Old Middle House, Malham Moor. An original two-bay house extended to three-bay, with later farm and cottage extensions.

Park House, Threshfield, 1640. Built in ashlar, it lacks an interesting wall texture.

Small cottage at Countersett, c. 1790. Two rooms, single storey.

**Above: Stone slate roofs,
Wensleydale.
Right: Cottage of 1679 at
Linton with three-light
mullioned window.**

Coping, kneeler, quoins and throughs on a barn at Blades, Swaledale.

4. Crucked Houses into Stone Houses

THE halls and tower houses represent the homes of the wealthy feudal lords of manors, feudal tenants and officials created by the Norman incomers from among their many attendant knights and companions and from a few of the Anglian headmen who submitted and became their vassals. The vast majority of the population was made up of the peasantry, most of them landless serfs with only a few of them free tenants and small farmers. The followers and attendants of the Norman barons found their accommodation about the castle premises and in sheds and tents in the castle bailey, living roughly as camp followers. Another class which had a provided accommodation in the twelfth and later centuries was the rapidly growing monastic population—monks, lay brethren and servants of the monasteries. The lay brethren were largely the builders and other craftsmen and some of the workers on the granges and monastic farms. The peasantry were largely left to themselves, to their own effort and ingenuity in the task of finding shelter. They could take small wood from the waste but not timber from the forest. They could devise their huts in crude fashion by fixing thin branches in the earth, drawing together their tops, binding them with withies and then making walls by intertwining smaller stuff. This wattle was then plastered with clay or mud to make "wattle and daub". The floor of such a hovel could be laid with rushes on trampled earth. In some parts their hovels could be made of clay lumps but there was little that could be called a house. Only the free tenants, the small farmers with a virgate or bovate tenure, with about ten or fifteen acres of land paid for by feudal services, were able to make something more substantial which could be called a cot or cottage. These were the buildings in which the "cruck" construction was used. A few crucked buildings have survived but their importance lies not in being a historic curiosity or rare survival, but in the influence they had in the evolution of the more permanent stone houses of which there are so many examples surviving in our villages. The cruck structure was introduced and used by the Anglo-Danish immigrants and some of the pre-Conquest houses were the prototype of the eleventh century small manor houses.

The cruck was a simple structural unit made with two matching curved beams got by splitting a slightly curved tree trunk or large branch lengthwise and then rough adzing the two halves to a rough rectangular section. The two beams were then set up as an arch with their tops together, with a short beam, the "collar", holding them together just below the top. A longer beam, the "tie", was fastened across about half way up like the stroke which made them into a strong and rough letter A. This was the completed "cruck" and two of them set up parallel at a distance of ten or twelve feet apart made "a pair of crucks". They were joined at the tops by the horizontal roof tree. If two straight beams were laid on the ends of the ties making a rectangular frame, the feet of the pair of crucks set about sixteen feet apart, it would be approximately a sixteen by twelve feet rectangle. This was a "bay" which remained the unit for building for several centuries. This was the traditional "bay's length" which had been determined at a very early date as the length in which two pair of oxen could have standing room and could turn. This was as early as 210 AD said by Pallodius the Roman architect to be about 16 ft. × 10 ft. and was also found to be practicable by the Anglo-Saxon builders. It was adopted because in the Anglo-Saxon manors the ox teams were put out in pairs to the tenants of the manor to be kept and cared for, and this measure, up to 18 feet between the cruck feet and 12 to 16 feet between the pair of crucks, ensured that a house of at least two pairs of crucks would accommodate a family in one and a pair of oxen in the second. These are most important measures as they dominated the Dales house plans right into the eighteenth century.

For many centuries the single bay was the extent of the peasant's house, but when he was able to improve his hovel as the Norman manors developed and the peasants shared in the common fields and had grazing on the commons for a cow or a few sheep, and some had to care for a pair of oxen for the common plough, the house could be extended by adding a pair of crucks and making an extension of a bay's length. The farms of the free tenants extended even to three and exceptionally to four bays. The feet of the crucks were set on large stones to prevent rot. Accounts for building a house at Kirkby Malham in 1454 include: "Also at erecting of the house of T. Paxton 4d. Also for drink given to the carpenter and for basyng the said houses that is to say for laying great stones under the foot of the Crokk 4d." The sides of the bay from ground level up to the wall plates (the horizontal beams on the tie ends) were filled in with a wall of sods or with wattle and daub. Thin branches, the "spars", laid with their feet on the wall plate and reaching to the ridge carried by the cruck tops, carried a thatch of rushes or heather. They were supported in the middle by a purlin scarfed to the crucks midway between tie and collar. The Kirkby Malham account includes the item "paid for thakke bought of T. Rakys and watlyng and thekkyng 2 houses entirely viz: his said dwelling house in Ayrton and the barn of the said house 18/4d.: also for thekkee bought and carriage to the barn of Tho. Paxton in Kirkby 8/-". The wattle and daub walls were sooner or later replaced by stone and, as large crucks which needed large trees were difficult to get and very costly, shorter crucks were used by footing them in the side wall, now strong enough to carry them. This can be seen in the High Laithe at Grimwith in Wharfedale, a crucked barn standing now on the edge of the reservoir.

Many of the cruck buildings were replaced in the seventeenth century by the new all stone houses, though a few cruck buildings still remain in the Barden area of Wharfedale. A few of the smaller cruck barns were altered directly with the side walls and gable ends of stone being kept. The stone gables sometimes show clearly where the steep slope of thatch has been changed to the flatter slope of stone slates by building up the side walls and filling in the triangle left between the two slopes with new walling.

There are some contemporary descriptions of the cruck houses which suggest that by the poorest modern standards they would be very crude and inadequate. Bishop Hall says of the small farmer's house that it is

Of one bay's breadth, God whot, a silly cot
Whose thatched spars are furred with sluttish soote
A whole inch thick, shining like Blackamoor's brows.
At his bed's feete feeden his stalled teame,
His swine beneath, his pullen oer the beame.

This emphasises a most important tradition, that with the peasant and small farmer his stock shared his house until the sixteenth century, when farm buildings for animals began to be built, although even then these were rare. The common evolution in the Dales was to build on extra bays and make a "long house" with bays at one end for the family living and the rest being housing for cattle, the separating mark between humans and stock being usually the doorway. The family part with its fireplace became known as the "firehouse", a name which persists in many seventeenth century deeds and conveyances. The fire had been moved in the crucked house from the middle of the floor to a place against the stone gable wall, and then to a fireplace built in a stone party wall between the two rooms of the new house or between the house and the laithe, when this party wall, taken up to the roof rigging, was strong enough to carry the weight of the chimney.

Crucked buildings remained in use even into the eighteenth century. In a survey of Cracoe in Wharfedale, which in part is of 1586 and part of 1603, there is the detail of many crucked buildings and also an account of small crofts which had been intaken from the waste of the manor. The tenants had been allowed by the Clifford lords of the manor "to make and repair their ancient firehouses and barns". Barns of two, three and four bays were built; "one firehouse and a lath (laithe) of three pair of crucks" was a typical cottage, one bay for the family and one for stock. A more wealthy small farmer built "a firehouse of four pair of crucks of oak and a barn and hay house each of two pair of crucks". Some houses were of oak and some of ash and one of three bays had a chamber over the wallplate of one bay, made by putting planks across the ties in the house part.

In an enquiry in 1603 into the extent of encroachments onto the waste in Cracoe we can recognise the beginning of the typical Dales house with its surrounding garth or small croft in which separate farm buildings began to be built. "Richard Blackburn hath improved one ffyrehouse and one other little house and a little garth in length ix yerdes and in breyd iiij yerde cessed to rent by yere 4d." George Girston had built his dwelling house on the lord's common and made a little garthing and an orchard 30 yards by 30 yards and his son had taken a little calf close of an acre and a rood and a half. In other villages the same was happening but more peasants were being freed from services and were becoming small farmers paying a rent instead. A survey in 1600 of Linton, Threshfield, Hetton, Flasby and Rilston lists many tenants with a house, a garth and one, two, or three bovates of land, the bovate generally fifteen acres. Rents varied from about eight to nineteen shillings a year. A survey of Ripley and Clint in 1635 lists 44 houses, many dating from the sixteenth century and all of cruck construction with wattle side walls. Some were of only two pairs of crucks but others were of three or four pairs and many of them had two or three more for shelter of cattle or hay. Most were thatched but three were partly slated. In Nidderdale there are at least seven crucked buildings remaining, although in some the crucks are concealed in later structures.

The change from timber crucked buildings to more substantial houses of stone started in the sixteenth century but became widespread when these small farmers began to prosper. Harrison in his *Description of England*, 1577, tells of these prosperous farmers, "every man turned builder, pulled downe the old house and set up a new after his owne devise". He was speaking of England as a whole but with a strong background of the Midlands and South and one could accept a delay of one or two generations of 25 or 30 years before his comments would apply generally to the North. It was nonetheless true that by the turn of the sixteenth-seventeenth centuries this replacement of old houses had begun and spread through all our villages during the seventeenth century. In the Midlands much of the new building was of fine timber-framed or "half-timber" houses which were of a new plan and style and were closely allied to the housing in the towns. They were built by a growing craft of professional carpenters and joiners in all but the smallest cottages. In the northern hilly districts there was an insufficient supply of long, strong timber for that style of new and larger house but there was no lack of good stone for walls and roofing slates.

A moderate number of masons and builders had been unemployed after the Dissolution of the monasteries and were wandering the countryside finding work on the many new bridges which were required as roads became busier and old bridges and fords became inadequate. It was natural that with their help available there should be initiated in the Dales a period of extensive stone building to which Harrison's "every man turned builder" might in part apply. No doubt a farmer prosperous enough to start on a new house could become his own builder, calling in the mason for such craftwork as windows and doorframes, and a carpenter for the roof and furnishings. It is likely that building would attract some young men as a new and thriving trade which they could enter by joining one or two masons or carpenters at first as labourers but gradually becoming more skilled men. The guilds were weakening and long apprenticeship was becoming rare in the rural areas.

These conditions provide the explanation of the widespread so-called "traditional houses" of the northern areas, which though differing from place to place in minor detail have a general similarity of form and plan. Tudor traditions embodied in the smaller manor houses of the sixteenth century lingered on and the general style in the seventeenth century stone houses retained something of a medieval appearance and plan. These houses are now being referred to as "vernacular architecture"—buildings belonging to the people as much as does their dialect. The new houses had no architect for their design nor did they follow any town or professional pattern—they were essentially a translation into and a replacement in stone of the two, three or four bay crucked house of the prosperous small farmer. No new plans were needed as the old house set the pattern—minor modifications could ensure a new standard of comfort and convenience. So far as the farmer was concerned it was incidental that this substitution of materials introduced new principles of construction which would continue to be applied to all kinds of

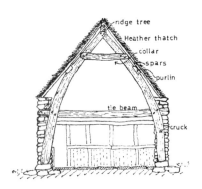
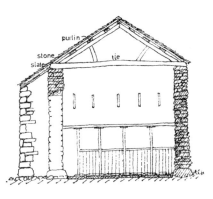

Relative positions of members in cruck and in stone-built laithe.

house even to today.

A limiting factor in cruck construction, based originally in pre-Conquest days on the room required for the accommodation of oxen, was in the hill country imposed by the lengths of available timber. The size of the bay, 12 ft. by 16 ft., could be spanned by purlins of 13 ft. and ties of 17 or 18 ft., but timbers longer than that would not be easy to get. If the cruck feet were set wider apart either the cruck would have to straddle at a flatter, weaker angle or longer timber would have to be found. The traditional timber lengths were closely governed by what was available near at hand. We have already seen that in building Bolton Castle longer timber had to be fetched from the Vale of Eden. The new houses were built to the old dimensions, but whereas the old crucks carried the weight of the roof, and walls could be mere wattle and daub, the cruck was now replaced by a roof truss resting its own weight and that of a stone roof on the wall top. The walls had replaced crucks as the load-bearing members. By making them substantial they could be carried high enough to make the loft space in the apex of the trusses into larger rooms with vertical walls spanned by a flatter triangular roof space. The flatter roof had shorter, stouter timbers, the rafters, which could carry a stone slate roof which was vastly more permanent and weather proof than thatch.

Internal party walls were built at the positions of some of the crucks and these were carried right up to the ridge to carry the roof tree and the purlins, other positions being taken by the intermediate trusses. These party walls divided the upper space for the first time into separate rooms of one or more bays' length. These upper rooms now had sufficient vertical wall for windows to be formed in it.

In the old tradition two or three bays were taken for the house part and two or three more for the cattle and hay. The house part was at first divided into a kitchen-living room, usually of two bays, and a parlour. A large fireplace was made on the gable wall or on the party wall if the kitchen did not lie next to the gable. It was essential that the wall which had the fireplace was strong enough to carry a heavy chimney structure. The parlour was often the bedroom of the master and mistress. The large rooms on the first floor would provide accommodation for the rest of the family and servants and some storage. In the larger houses a dairy might be made by a single bay extension at the end if the living room—just called "the house"—was there, or made by building an offshut, lean-to at the back of the house. The offshut, taken the length of the building, could provide back kitchen or scullery as well as a dairy, and could allow of a wider cow house in the rest. When the kitchen came next to the farm part, there was usually a door between it and the cow house so that animals could be served without having to go outside. One or two bays might be made for a hay barn and so the "long house" of traditional pattern had evolved. It is perhaps paradoxical to remember that much of its style, plan and dimensions were determined by the size of timber in the pre-Conquest North and by the requirements of a pair of oxen.

The plan was capable of variations in the allocation of rooms among the many bays and offshut area. With offshuts the roof slope was unaltered, but was carried down in a continuous slope so that offshuts are generally only one storey high. In looking at these houses a wallhead can often be seen where a parlour or dairy has been added, the wall head marked sometimes by one set of quoins on the original house end.

In the new house two features take on a new shape. The ladder access to the loft over the ties, generally referred to as being "on the balks", was replaced by a stone staircase. This was sometimes placed on the back wall, never as in more recent housing rising from somewhere near the house door. Often it was a part spiral rising on one side of the fireplace or placed in a projection from the back wall of the house. This projecting feature can still be seen in some old Dales houses. The fireplace was still the focal point of the social life of the family. The "ingle nook", a sentimental name of little significance, was an adaptation to provide for the burning of logs and branches. The wide fireplace was spanned by an arch which carried a large canopy sometimes extending into the room above, in which canopy or "beef loft" beef and mutton was hung to be smoked. In the eighteenth and

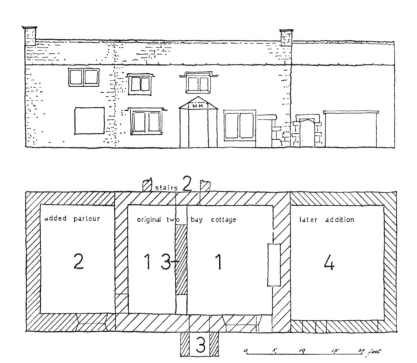

nineteenth centuries the fine mason work of this arch was replaced by a plain straight lintel of less span, and the whole framed a cast iron fire range. In the seventeenth century house the arch may have a span of eight or more feet and a depth inside it of three feet. The side wall towards the door was sometimes extended either in stone or wood as a partition, the "hack", against which a settle was placed secured from draughts. A settle often faced it on the other side and made a small cosy room of the fireplace.

The chimney was a massive structure which had to be progressively narrowed from the arch to the base of the final chimney stack at roof level. In some houses, and more commonly in the western dales, to carry the great weight of a massive chimney, it was built up from ground level, protruding from the gable wall. Sometimes an internal fireplace hood turns through the wall into a short final stack carried partly in and partly outside the gable on a set of corbels. This makes a very attractive feature to be seen in Dentdale and Garsdale and commonly in Westmorland.

48

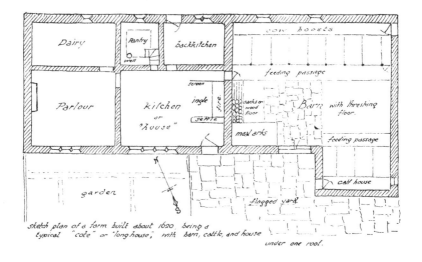

Above: Sketch plan of a typical "long house", c. 1620.
Left: Order of building of Old Middle House, Malham Moor (see also photograph on page 37).

Long houses were not necessarily built at a single time. Some started out as a plain two or three bay house on the old cruck plan. Extra bays and farm bays were added as sons married or the farm prospered, and wall heads show these additions. By the mid-seventeenth century the addition of service rooms in a single storey offshut at the back, and a porch at the front, sometimes with a date to it, became fairly common. In most houses a careful and critical examination will reveal something much more than a simple story of building and the house will be seen to have grown by a series of events. Where there is a date on a doorhead, usually with the initials of man and wife, commonly arranged with the surname initial over the christian initials of the two, it is sometimes the date of building, or of a marriage or it may be later belonging to an inheritance and alteration. Again careful study will generally show the relation of the date to the period of the growth of the house to which it belongs.

The stone walls of the house were load bearing but the load was very much increased in stone slated roofed buildings. Only a very small part of the roof load was carried by the spar feet onto the wallplates. The party walls were carried up to gable

49

height and so some of the purlins could rest on them with the bulk of the roof weight resting on the spars which in turn were bedded on the purlins. The part of the outer wall between the trusses or party walls, that is in each bay, was carrying only its own weight and could be broken by window and door openings. At first the windows were small, generally of two lights. Mullions were put in to separate the two lights, but of greater necessity to support the lintel which carried the weight of the wall above the opening. In· the absence of mathematical theory this would be imagined as the weight of all the wall right to the roof; the idea of a bearing arch bringing much of this load onto the side mullions would not be appreciated. It was natural to prop up the lintels with short and sturdy mullions which were regarded as load carrying struts.

The provision of mullions and doorheads presented what was possibly the greatest problem in the gathering of materials for a house. While walling stone, flags and slates could be got at many horizons in nearly all the geological groups of rocks, in which there were many small quarries, stone from which long and strong struts—mullions—and beams for lintels and doorheads could be cut were few and far between. The skilled cutting and heavy cost of transport made these special stones expensive. In the houses of the early seventeenth century the windows often look very low, even if they are long and of three, four or five lights, two lights being the most common. This is because of the great expense of longer mullions. Lintels were something of a problem, as these were moulded and in long windows were generally arranged to be propped by mullions. One or two long bearers, usually of thick flags were laid over them to break joints for the walling above them. In early houses these are the only carved and moulded items which needed the skill of a mason as distinct from a waller or builder. The quarry at Greets on the ridge above Castle Bolton is one in the strong bed of the Ten Fathom Grit from which mullions, lintels and quoins could be cut, and these were sent to many parts of the Dales.

In a few places lintels and sills have been cut out of thick, good quality flags, this being more often the case in Dentdale and Garsdale where more massive stone is scarce. These flags are often placed double and sometimes with the top one projecting one or two inches to form a primitive drip mould which, though simple, can be very effective both in its function and as a feature. These are seen mostly on farm buildings. In many Dales buildings the doorway opening is a simple structure of three stones, two jambs and a lintel, but these are nearly all buildings of eighteenth or nineteenth century date. Until the massive rock of the Millstone Grit was made available by more skilful quarrymen and stone cutters, and ways of transport were considerably improved, these monolithic jambs were too expensive for the small building. With the development of the stone saw in the late eighteenth century, the Georgian architects made great use of smooth sawn sections to frame their much larger, vertical-rectangular windows and for their doorways and porches with pediments. It was this fashion and material which was copied and used by the late eighteenth and nineteenth century builders of larger houses who could employ an architect.

In the seventeenth century the doorways were framed with several roughly matching stones on each side, which were brought to a squared edge with a true face worked on upper and lower sides for setting. The stones, usually five or sometimes seven on each jamb, were a long oblong shape, set alternately with length horizontal and vertical. The horizontal ones, sometimes called stretchers made the bottom and top ones and a middle one, these three separated by two risers placed vertical. The bottom stone on each side was usually larger than the others and made a good plinth by projecting a little. The opening was spanned by a heavy lintel, deeper than it was thick. Usually a moulding, at first a simple chamfer, later more complex, was carried round the two sides and across the lintel or head stone and much local variety is to be seen in these mouldings, both in different areas and at different dates. They can provide a study in themselves that will be found very rewarding. A comparable squaring of stones larger than the walling stones is seen making the corners of the building, where similar stones are set "long and short" making a carefully worked and shaped corner. These are the quoins. They may be given sufficient prominence, standing a little proud of the wall face, and become a decorative feature of the house. This is particularly the case in the later building and is an important feature in most Georgian houses.

Two other places give some scope for a little ornament but as these are functional features, chimneys and gables, the ornament is at a minimum. The roof slates are carried to the outer face of the gable to give weather protection to the top of the gable wall and may be made to overlap the wall by an inch or more. A common sixteenth and seventeenth century practice however was to lay on top of the slates over the gable wall and, as wide as its thickness, a coping of carefully cut fine flagstone. This broad strip of flags was brought down to a large stone at the head of the quoins, and this was long enough, being well built into the wall, to project over the front as a corbel. The projecting part was moulded, sometimes in the later buildings with a very complicated moulding. It was shaped so that the coping flags butted against it at the back and it could take any thrust they might have. In larger buildings the kneelers, as the stones were called, carried an ornament on them—a ball (rarely), a small moulded spike or something more elaborate.

Chimneys cannot be anything but prominent so in most yeoman houses some attempt was made to make them at least of neat and acceptable design. A very common form has a slightly wider plinth section astride the roof ridge, chamfered on its top edge. Above this the chimney shaft is built of thick flags set on edge. They are so cut to size that four will generally make the rectangle of the shaft, each face showing the length of one flag and the thickness of the flag of the next side. The next set of flags are placed to overlap the other way so that the long flag comes over the end section of the one below and meets the edge of its mate over the long flag below. This will be clear in the photograph. Usually not more than three or four "rings" of flags make the shaft, then a collar of narrow flags with a moulded edge is laid, and above that another "ring" of much narrower flags. If this pattern is not used, the chimney shaft may be built as ordinary walling, with a flag collar, but it has nothing like the same handsome appearance. This is about the only place in good building where "face bedding", that is stone set on its edge and not on its natural bed, would be tolerated. Stone set this way soon deteriorates with frost and will split or peel off in blisters in time. This can be appreciated by the large number of chimneys one sees which for this reason have been built in ordinary walling, many of them rebuilt at a time when the edge stones have begun to break up. In the western dales this form of chimney is rare and circular ones, quite massive, are built of small stone properly laid.

5.   A Yeoman builds his House

THE traditional "long" house with a plan closely following that of the crucked building was essentially the combined house and farmstead of the newly emerging class of yeoman farmers. At the Dissolution of the monasteries the estates were sold to landed gentry and established families like the Earls of Cumberland who bought much of the Bolton Priory estate, or to wealthy London merchants like the Greshams who bought much of Fountains property. These owners quickly sold farms and small properties to the tenants already on them, either for cash or mortgage. It was these new owners who after two or three generations of the Elizabethan prosperity were able to afford a new house. Plenty of masons had become available from the town and mansion rebuilding and in most areas peasants who had been hired to labour for mason gangs had picked up enough skill to make building an ordinary house seem possible. In the Dales good stone was of wide occurrence and almost every village has the remains of one or more small quarries on the edge of the waste of the manor. This was so much the case that nearly all the enclosure awards of the eighteenth and nineteenth centuries assign the traditional quarry as the "township quarry", for the use of the township for building and repairs. Some of these quarries are now almost forgotten, a few expanded into large commercial ventures, many are overgrown or are now being disguised by the tipping of rubbish, but all can be found with a little care. It is the variety of stone in these different quarries which has given the charming variations to a traditional style and common plan which, if carried out in identical material, say brick, could have become very monotonous. We might now ask what was the normal procedure when the decision had been made that a new house should be built.

First let us look more closely than we have done at the materials which would be required for the new building and see how they could be got together. We can leave the cost for the present though no doubt it would have a prime place in the deliberations of the yeoman whose new house we are thinking about. The first obvious requirement was stone but, although we have shown that there are very many small quarries scattered through the Dales, a little thought will show that more than one kind of stone would be required. The walls were to keep out the weather and also carry the considerable load of a stone-covered roof, and they were generally between two and three feet thick. The foundations to carry these heavy structures were made strong but not laid very deep. Large boulders from the land clearance were often used, up to two or three feet in length. These were fitted in a double row of footings in a shallow trench which went little deeper than the subsoil. This footing was carefully laid and all the spaces in it made up with firmly placed boulders. In some areas glacial moraine boulders would be numerous enough to supply some of the plainer walling, though building with these called for special skill. If the walling stone, as was usually the case, was got from the local quarry it could vary within wide limits. In general terms within the area of the Yoredale Series of rocks, in which flaggy sandstones are very frequent and associated with almost every limestone, a good source of walling stones was in any thicker beds of flag, say about four or more inches. These flags could be cut by a mason, or by others with a bit of patience and practice, into fairly regular stones. These would have a good natural bed and top and, with one good edge for face, were easy to build with. The many flagstones within the Yoredales, however, are by no means uniform and the different beds of them vary in thickness, colour, grain size and texture on the break. So, according to where the house was being built the whole texture and appearance of its walls could be different. A comparison of almost any newer house in Burtersett, with its thin, rather drab stones of the Burtersett flags from below the Middle Limestone, with some further down the dale say at Askrigg where a building stone below the Hardraw Scar Limestone has been used, which is of a much brighter colour and more robust, and which is cut to more varied sizes, will demonstrate this first most important feature, the variety of wall-texture.

In the earlier and bigger buildings it had been part of the work of the masons to open a quarry and to get their own stone. To save carriage this was usually as near as possible, so buildings are very local in the character of their main walls. It was a new widespread demand for stone ready cut to size that brought the new craftsman, the quarryman, in the nineteenth century. In the eighteenth century he was not yet a man working all his time in the quarry but often a small farmer or such who had the necessary knowledge to go out, get and prepare stone either in the common quarry or in a small one which he could lease. If a particularly fine finish or a special appearance was wanted, then stone might be brought from a special quarry but this involved the difficulties of transport and cost and perhaps some special arrangement to get stone from a different township.

In some parts of the Dales the Millstone Grit was the dominant rock, and this provided flags near its base, most of which were more robust than the Yoredales, thicker and harder. These took more working and were cut to more "blocky" sizes. Many "lifts" (separate layers) in the Millstone Grit were not flaggy, and then more massive beds could be handled only by skilled stone cutters who produced walling stones of very regular size suited to the proper working of the stone. Some beds were suited for gateposts and other heavy work.

This is true in the south-east of the Dales, particularly of some buildings in Wharfedale south and east from Burnsall where quarries on the north flank of the Barden Fell mass of Millstone Grit have been used. The quarries on the other parts of the fell supplied Skipton Castle and much of the later building in the Skipton, Eastby and Embsay areas. This question of wall texture dependent on the size, proportions, regularity and colour of the stones cannot be over emphasised. It must be remembered also that where boulder material is sufficiently abundant the walls may be rubble built with stones of varied size and shape including both sandstones and limestones and flaggy throughs. If well built, random rubble walling can be very attractive.

In Ribblesdale and the south-west area of the Dales the Yoredale sandstones are not present and the Millstone Grit occurs mainly to the south towards Bowland. The stones of easiest access are the true slates and grits of the pre-Carboniferous, the Silurian to pre-Cambrian, Horton Flags, Studfold Sandstone, Conistone Flags and the Ingletonian series. These have all been quarried and used along with the massive Great Scar Limestone, this latter rock mainly in the form of land clearance boulders. The true slates and flags of these beds are more massive than those of the Yoredales and their fracture is irregular so that they break with a jagged end or sharp spiky pieces. As walling stone they are similar to the slates so widely used in the Lake District to which they are closely allied in geological age. They are nearly all a good greeny-blue colour, are often walled "dry" and are usually very attractive.

In Dentdale and Garsdale much of the building has been done with rather thicker Yoredale flags quarried at the head of Deepdale in the strata above the Middle Limestone and in Scotcher Gill from flags below the same limestone. These two areas have supplied most of the building in Dentdale, and quarries in Garsdale at the same horizons have been used there. The use of some fashions copied from Westmorland building, particularly the round and corbelled chimneys, gives Dentdale and Garsdale a character of their own which is recognisably different in many minor details from that of the other dales.

Different stone was used in some other parts of the house from that used in the main walling. The ground floor was paved with flags and these needed to be substantial, two or even more inches thick, large to avoid as many dirt-harbouring cracks as possible, fine grained for smoothness and of a good colour which would improve with sanding and scrubbing. Some of the finest of these qualities are found in the Horton Flags of Helwith Bridge, and these were used in most of upper Ribblesdale and were carried into Malhamdale, over into Littondale and some even into Dentdale. In other dales the heavier flags from the flags below the Middle Limestone at Carperby, which were of large size and hard, and those from the base of Millstone Grit from Birkdale, were very widely used. These were quarries with a high reputation. In Wharfedale there was no native flagstone of comparable quality but some of the quarries around Keighley were not too far away, if specially good quality were desired. Usable flag could be got at Embsay and Rilston for everyday hard wearing. Some other flags of special quality were "firestone" that neither crumbled nor splintered when fire was used on or near them. Large and heavy firestones were used for hearthstones and thinner ones were used for bakestones for oatcake making, which were found in many houses of the eighteenth century. Firestones were also used for chimneys which were exposed to heat inside and extreme weather outside, which put ordinary thin flag to great stress. The name Baxton Gill, Backstone Edge and many other variants marks places where good quality flags for this purpose could be got. Other large and good quality flags were needed for dairy and milk house shelves and for this purpose Horton Flags were long a favourite. Considerable care and knowledge was called for in choosing the flags used in a farm house.

A special problem in the walling was the framing of openings, doorways and windows, the strengthening of the walls with throughs and the binding of the corners of the building with quoins. The usual structure of the walls was an outer and an inner skin well built and the space between these made up with well placed rubble. The face walls were tied together with flaggy throughs which were laid across the whole width of the wall. In farm buildings the ends of the throughs often stick out beyond the wall, but in house walls the stones are trimmed off to fit like the rest of the wall. The throughs need to be long and very strong and a few quarries became known for the quality of their throughs. A quarry at Cow Close above Litton supplied good throughs to many parts of Wharfedale.

The rectangular openings for windows and doorways needed

well defined and strong sides, and a beam-like top to carry the load of the wall above it, though this was not as big as the seventeenth century builders thought. For the top of the doorway the necessary strength, if a suitable stone could be got, would be found by giving it more depth than thickness. Probably three or three and a half feet long, two feet high and twelve to eighteen inches thick, would be chosen. The best rock with the necessary strength would be found in the Millstone Grit. For maximum strength the doorheads and lintels should be laid "on bed" and this required them to be cut from beds thick enough to give their necessary height. As explained before, the window lintels could be of more than one section, supported by the mullions, and as the mullions were in compression they could be cut with their length along and not across the bed, so their grain is at right angles to that of the lintels and sills. The early side mullions were moulded only on one side. The other side, built into the wall, was often very irregular, but later in the seventeenth century the mullions were properly squared and moulded, giving a much better finish to the windows.

The making of the doorway sides with cut verticals and stretchers and the use of "long and short" in the quoins has been explained in the previous chapter (page 51). The coping sometimes placed over the gable wall-head was for weather protection and had no load to carry so any good and thin flagstones would do, often got from some quarry for roofing slates. The roofing slates were not slate in the geological sense, of rocks formed under pressure and with an imposed cleavage, but were very thin bedded flags from one or two horizons in the Yoredales and from beds near the base of the Millstone Grit. They needed to be durable and frost resistant, not liable to further splitting and preferably smooth grained, not giving much hold to moss and lichen. Smooth slates would lie well and also look well and at the same time were easier to make weather proof. Coarser and cheaper slates were used on outhouses and some farm buildings, for instance those from the Grassington Grit of Slatepit Rigg, widely used in Wharfedale on second class building, but for a house it was a matter of pride to get a better quality. Many slates were got from Starbotton Fell, Walden Head, from Nidderdale—Scot Gate Ash quarries and some others —and from several flag beds around the Dales, but the best came out of Coverdale and from Hill Top, Birkdale and Stags Fell near Hawes, with only a few other quarries. In the big quarries of Coverdale, Carperby, Burtersett, Stags Fell and a few others, the slates were mined underground and brought out to daylight in large blocks. These were set up to weather over a winter after which they split easily. The splitting and cutting to a great variety of sizes used on a single roof was done in sheds on the quarry floor by banker hands. This separation of quarrymen (miners) and bankers was a feature of the nineteenth century. In the seventeenth and eighteenth centuries of which we are now speaking the quarries were small without underground working and the same man was quarryman and banker hand. Given notice he would get and cut the required slates or flags for a given size of roof or room from material that had already partly weathered in his open quarry floor. In most available accounts the slates and stone were bought at the quarry and brought to an agreed point at which the builder could collect them or arrange the transport.

It will make all this detail more easily appreciated if some of it is illustrated from the accounts for the building of an actual home in the Dales. Notes on the cost of building a few houses, barns and extensions to houses have fortunately been preserved and are worth close study. A traditional, old house in Conistone was partly rebuilt and extended by Richard Wigglesworth in the year following from October 1685 and he kept accounts of the whole transactions, though they are scattered in no particular order among other notes in a day book and in other casual places. They would apply to most traditional houses so we may look at some of them in detail. As a freeholder of the manor, Wigglesworth had the right to fetch building stone from the township quarry on Out Moor at the cost only of getting, carting and paying the nominal lord's rent. The township quarries were on Bycliffe in the Millstone Grit, two miles away, but there was a sledge track down to the village. From odd notes it becomes clear that the stone was got in rough lumps at the quarry and a mason on the building site cut it to whatever stone size he needed. In one of the farm buildings to be built, for instance:

"Howebeck Leath let to build with Tho. Kidd for £3 & is to make it eleaven yards in length within & five yards in breadth & seaven yards in breadth in ye shippon and fower yards high to ye square (eaves) & to break all ye greet (grit) stone and to hew one door". "Thos. Kidd hath taken ye laith to wall at ye rate of sixpence ye yard and is to break (cut) all ye hewen stones in at ye bargain for one rough arch & ye corner stones (quoins) and hath received sixpence in earnest being December ye 27 1685."

It is also seen from these two statements that the earlier custom of giving the builder only the general dimensions and leaving him to know what detail he should build still applied.

Slates for the roof were ordered well in advance from a quarry in October: —

"That Thomas Harrison hath sould Twenty gaiges of sleat unto me and is to deliver it good and sufficient to ye sight of any workman between ye first day of May next ensuing ye date hereof for Two pounds & ten shillings but ye said Richard Wigglesworth is to pay ye chief lord his dues".

It is seen that the quarryman was given six months to the delivery date in which to get, weather, split and shape the slates. They were then to be delivered, led down from "ye hard raike in Waldenhead" to Starbotton and to be set down on the Conistone side of the mill bridge. John Simonson would find a place for them to lie and for this part of the carriage they were to have a crown a gaige. John Harrison and John Calvert were to have 6s. a gaige delivered as the other was, and half a peck of malt. These were not all the slates brought from Walden Head but later and smaller parcels were fetched for outbuildings and barns.

The complex business of laying a roof with the graded sizes of stone slates from eaves to ridge has been described in other places.* The change from a thatched to a stone roof had two effects—the slope was made less, an angle of 30° being the most on which slates could be made secure, and the great weight of them needed much stronger timbers and better roof trusses. To get truss members of the required length and strength it might be necessary to buy trees in some distant woodland and have them felled and cut up there. The scarcity and great expense of long timber encouraged the continuance of the traditional narrow dimensions of the crucked house which had been related always to the most available size of timber.

Like the slates, timber was ordered well in advance by Wigglesworth. He arranged to select and buy some standing trees in Barden Forest twelve miles away and he

"paid to Sampson Lupton for two trees 4.15.0
paid more to Sampson Lupton towards three trees 0. 5.0
for felling fower trees & in ale 2 one day and 3 one day 0. 6.0
for quartering & cutting one great tree 0. 4.0
to Christopher Broadbelt for cutting a great tree 0. 1.0
in ale when we led the wood from Greenor Hill 0. 1.8
paid to Jo Ellis & Wm West for sawing .... 0.10.0."

The sawing up of the trees was done at Barden and again Wigglesworth fetched it from there to Conistone. At the same time he needed much more prepared timber and this he bought from John Piccard of Keighley

"eighty sparres or upwards—so many as shall suffice for a house of 19 yards in length and 21 yards of roofe trees 4 inches square and spares 4 inches deep and 3 inches in thickness for 1s. 1½d. a piece & roof trees to be delivered at ye same price according to there length & all of them to be sufficient to the sight of a workman and to be delivered between (now) and ye michaelmas come twelve months at Barden Scale and ye Broadparke & 6d. in earnest paid."

---

* Walton, *Homesteads of the Yorkshire Dales*, Dalesman, 1947, 41-46.
Raistrick, A., *Grey Roofs*, *Out of Doors*, 1946, 32-34.

It is clear from this that **Piccard** was a sawyer who would cut up and prepare the timber already quartered and get it ready at Barden Scale. More timber was got in other places:

"Two Balkes bought of aforesaid John Piccard which is to be delivered a foot square throughout & 18 foot in length in Middleton Woof in a place where it is sufficient for a Draught to come to it for fifteen shillings a piece & is to be paid at Michaelmas next when ye Balkes is delivered."

This contract was made at Anthony Naylor's house at Skipton and William West of Conistone with Anthony Naylor was to check the quality of all material when it was delivered. The skeleton of the roof was now provided for, rooftree, wall plates, timber for trusses and so on. For the slating spars and laths, and blacksmiths wares, Piccard was to provide:

"80 sparres & 5 eastres pieces & 2 balkes for 6. 0.0
paid for lat nails & spikings May ye 18 .... 0. 8.0
paid for one hundred of latts ye same time 0. 4.0
paid for 3 hundred of latts ye 11th November 0.12.6
paid to George Lowcock June ye 14th ye sum of £4 in pte for
14 sparres & 1,000 lattes 45s. & ribbes & one mould board."

Some of these laths were used on barns for which the accounts were not always clearly separated. All the laths were to be riven, that is split not cut, by Robert Wiggon.

The materials for the main structure now being provided and assembled, building proceeded and was done by Thomas Johnson, Thomas Harrison and James Stackhouse, all paid for "walling ye house". Thomas Green was paid for "dressing ye slates". Flags for the ground floor were bought from Joseph Motley at some other quarry than the slates and cost 19 shillings. Daniel Tailforth was paid £2 for making "6 windows & 4 lowpholes and one double piped chymney". Thomas Kidd may have been employed on the house as he was on the barn to cut all the hewn stones for the quoins and an arch. The account for this special mason work and a few other items may have been on some of the several missing pages of the Day Book. Wood for floors, 13 fir deals and one Norway oak were bought and John Elles and Thomas Sergeantson were paid for sawing them into planks, but there is no note of where they were bought.

Many other entries refer to the joiner making "joined" furniture, doors and ceilings. The blacksmith made snecks, hinges and other ironwork. The wages of 6d. a day paid to the wallers amount to 236 days and if all three worked all the time the building took about five weeks for the walls. The total of the surviving accounts is £74 8s. 9d. and so it might be a reasonable estimate to say the house cost about £100.

Wigglesworth's accounts continue with much detail of furnishings, curtains, bedding, cupboards and crockery, silver, pewter and so on which hardly come into the theme of building. The contents of many seventeenth and eighteenth century houses are to be found listed in the inventories attached to wills. Some of these show us what rooms these new houses had, and a very average one is that of Robert Swale of Hartforth who died in 1662. His house had a forehouse with tables, leather chairs and a fire range which is the usual parlour; the buttery had tables, dresser, chairs, glass cupboard, pots, dishes and so on, so would be the "house" or living room. The milkhouse or dairy had tables, shelves and milk vessels, and there was a kitchen with table, dresser shelves and stools. Rooms over the parlour and buttery were store rooms; those over the kitchen and milkhouse were bedrooms and there were garrets with beds for the servants.

The accounts of the Conistone house can be matched with many fragments for others which are sufficient to enable us to accept them as typical of the way in which many of the houses of the seventeenth century yeomen were built. Harrison said that these men pulled down their old house and turned builder. There are a few examples of this. In another smaller house in Wharfedale, Howlebank House, a mason was paid for pulling down the house and then for rebuilding it. Slates were bought but the old stone and timber were re-used. Another account for Hillcastle House includes a payment "for ridding groundwork and pulling downe ye olde house. . . . for six dayes meat and wages fower shillings". Two gaiges of slates were bought from the quarry and a mason was paid for walling. Separate payment was made for getting, leading and cutting corner stones and flags. James Stackhouse was paid "for sleating ye laithe porch and Hillcastle house, 3s., getting ling and leading & Thatching at Hillcastle house thirty shilling". The balks and bowses in the old leath (laith) were sold for £2. In both buildings the stone and some timber were re-used and only quoin and arch stones were got new. The house except the porch may have been thatched to avoid buying stronger timber.

A valuable insight into the activity of some of the farmers in the rebuilding in Swaledale is afforded by the diaries left by the family of Garth of Crackpot and Summer Lodge where for several generations they farmed. Between April 1795 and 1905 members of the family kept a continuous daily note of the work done. The daily entries are seldom more than a very brief statement of the nature of the work with occasional comment on the weather. They contain no note on prices, quantities or locations except by an occasional name—work is described by the name of the person for whom it was done. For the first six months entries are made each day for Richard and Francis separately and it appears that Francis was more consistently at work on the farm or with a lime kiln, and Richard did more varied work at the farm, building and at quarries. For example common entries are (Francis) "Dressing manure"; (Richard) "at Thwaite with hay"; or (Richard) "at quarry". The farm routine is fully shown. Spring had the leading of manure, ploughing, sowing oats, potatoes and sometimes turnips; harvest was mainly hay making with a reaping of oats and later lifting of potatoes and turnips. There was constant interest in cattle breeding, pigs were kept, a few horses, and sheep after the enclosures. The full year's routine is there.

For our purpose, however, Richard's other activities are more relevant. He had a quarry and worked in several others according to where he was building. His work as a slater and waller gradually got precedence over his building, though all his life he continued to do building repairs. He did most of his own carpentry, felling trees and sawing them up for his timbers, making gates and doors and other carpentry things. For each particular job he generally employed one or two men by the day to work with him but did not seem to employ a permanent labourer.

His work shows that many farm buildings were in a very poor condition and could occasionally be repaired, but more often had to be replaced. It becomes clear that many of the laithes, cowhouses and barns which we now know were rebuilt in this way. We can take a few examples out of many in the diaries which will make the course of this rebuilding clear. Every day's entry occurs in strict calendar course, and sometimes a single job extends in odd days over months. However, we will start with one which is fairly quickly completed.

1795 April 22 to 25, pulling down cowhouse at Thwaite.
       May 3 to 9, 14 to 21, 25, 26, walling at Thwaite (rebuilding).
       May 27, 29, rearing timbers (putting roof trusses on).
       June 12, 13, dressing slate (at quarry).
       June 14, sawing laths.
       June 15 to 19, burning lime.
       June 15 to 19, slating.
       July 7 to 9, slating.   Had John Whitfield total 21 days.

In September he pulled down the Schoolroom (? Reeth), was cutting foundations, then walling 16 days with Robert and John Whitfield helping him for eleven days. Other days had been spent at the quarry and "in Swale" and in leading stones. As many of his jobs have "in Swale" and "leading stones" coming together it suggests that stones from the very extensive gravel banks of the Swale were used for rubble walling, and better stone, throughs and slates were got from the quarries. Often there is a similar sequence of entries:

      March 30, propping Geo. Calvert's Cowhouse.
      April 2, pulling down Geo. Calvert's Cowhouse.

Then, between April 7 and May 1 were intermittent days of walling at the Cowhouse. In July he was propping Eglon's Cowhouse, then pulling it down, getting and leading stone and walling in the next two weeks. Hay making and mowing then took July 23 to August 21 and the Eglin's barn was then finished on August 31. One more example may be quoted. Between September 22 and October 3 he had spent three days pulling down Nettlebed House. He then worked some days in the quarry and dressed "window stones" and "chimney top stones" and did some walling. Then the east end of the house was pulled down and there was a longish spell of intermittent walling, then setting fireplace and chimney and beam filling and plastering followed, and the house was finished in November. A milkhouse was walled concurrently and one of the very rare mentions of quantities is that the slates on the house measured three roods (147 square yards) and on the milkhouse 17 square yards. As in most cases the pulling down only took two or three days, we can assume that many crucked buildings were thatched, and that some of the timbers were cut and re-used in the new slated roof, as only occasionally did he fell a tree and cut new timbers.

During the next fifteen years the Garth family continued to rebuild cowhouses and barns and to repair and occasionally rebuild houses. Richard built a few small bridges and did a lot of field walling. Especially as Enclosure Awards were given or enclosure agreed for common pastures and moors, he spent much time putting up division fence walls. In his quarry he still hewed and "dressed" stone, slates, flags and gateposts. A proportion of wall stone was got from the Swale. His principal quarries were in the Gill (Summer Lodge Gill), Dalehead, Jackson's (Thwaite) and Sunside (Crackpot). Others were at Barf (Healaugh), Bigg-slack, Swinnergill, Satronside, Muker Edge and occasionally he fetched slate from others including Stagsfell. For some years he leased Jackson's quarry and sold stone which was mined there, and there are references to men being paid to drive the level and maintain it. He was quite an accomplished surveyor often employed in "dialling" for the mines, laying out Enclosure Divisions and walls, and in miscellaneous surveys for farmers.

As the Garths prospered they got an interest in some of the mines, Crackpot Moor and Whitaside, both near their home, and Loanin End beyond Keld. For several years Richard was agent for one of the Tan Hill collieries and for the Cotterdale Pit. He developed a business in supplying timber to the mines, did some shaft lining with timber, and had either a carpenter's shop or had access to one at Gunnerside where he cut a good deal of crib timbers for mines, turned wheel naves, and at one time made a new axle for a water wheel and walled the water wheel pit. In the early years of the nineteenth century he became

63

interested in planting and, between attending fairs from Bedale to Brough in the course of his cattle breeding and trading, he did sufficient tree planting to leave an important change on part of Swaledale. He joined John Birkbeck and went frequently to a nursery at Cotherstone where he bought many parcels of two and three year old trees. A typical "parcel" in 1811 is one of over 18,000—11,000 larch, 7,000 Scotch fir, and a mixed bundle of birch, beech and sycamore.

Later generations of the Garths reduced the quarry and mine interests but did not extinguish them. Building was still undertaken occasionally but by the later years of the nineteenth century their time was taken up with County Council, local authority, charity, school board and committee work of all kinds and labourers were permanently employed to manage the farm. Richard Garth had been in some respects typical of several men of his time spread about the Dales—men who could get stone in the quarries, build with it and do the necessary carpentry. They developed into quarrymen or builders, continuing for two or three generations. The Maxfield family of Grassington have been a team of builders continuing for more than a century; the Brennands are still represented in Skipton by a member who is a builder and works in much of the southern dales; Peacocks of Wensleydale have continued quarry and building traditions and there are still similar families in most of the Dales.

Many of the farmers having completed their buildings and created the farm yard turned their attention before the First World War to building themselves a new house. This was usually in solid four-square style, substantial and convenient rather than ornate, but acceptable as part of the rural scene. Much more difficult to assimilate but now with us to stay are the modern prefabricated buildings on a much larger scale than the old stone structures. Most problematic is the upstanding finger of the tall silo towers, and the planners will have to find ways of integrating these new forms into the existing farm groupings until we can accept them as naturally as we accepted the tall chimneys which were brought into the Dales with some of the mills and smelt mills of the nineteenth century.

Friar Head, Winterburn, an Elizabethan mansion of c. 1590. (Photo: Bertram Unné.)

Old Hall, Linton, with Georgian wing replacing end bays of a 17th century Dales house, c. 1750.

Linton Hospital, 1721-5. Vanbrugh, Palladian with Georgian windows and projecting quoins in the gables. (Photo: Bertram Unné.)

Gable of Linton Hospital, built of ashlar with window surrounds, projecting quoins and pediment, all a foretaste of Georgian style.

Small Georgian house at Yockenthwaite, Langstrothdale, with broad extension at left. Plain surrounds to windows, pedimented doorway and prominent quoins.

Elizabethan hall at Askrigg, destroyed by fire in 1936. (Photo: Wilfred Moore.)

Georgian detail of early 18th century at West Witton. Windows with "Gibb's surrounds", string courses round the house, quoins prominent, bearing arch over the wide window, and coping and kneeler on gable corner.

Cottage at Linton. Right half, 1641, with mullioned windows, string course hood-mould, doorhead with recessed spandrils and wall of coursed rubble. Left half 19th century addition with random rubble wall and tall windows, flag framed.

Friends' Meeting House, Brigflatts, near Sedbergh, 1675. The part left of the porch is the caretaker's house.

A country school — Threshfield Grammar School, 1675.

Methodist Chapel of 1873 at Carlton in Coverdale, built of local stone but with tiled roof.

The Powder House, Langthwaite, Arkengarthdale, c. 1804.

Commercial limekiln, Greenhow Hill, late 19th century.

Limekiln at Whaw, Arkengarthdale.

The Great Octagon lead-smelting mill at Langthwaite, Arkengarthdale, seen in the process of demolition. (Photo: J. A. Carpenter.)

Gayle cotton mill, Wensleydale, 1787.

6. Mansion, Cottage and Farmstead

THE period of rebuilding was approximately the century from 1650 to 1750 when the occupations of quarryman, mason and builder began to separate and be defined and the materials were more frequently provided by the builder who bought stone at the quarry ready prepared to the sizes he wanted, employing his own mason for all the special cutting. The carpenter was employed by him and got his timber from the saw mill or timber merchant. The joiner was moving towards the status of joiner and cabinet maker and in almost every trade specialisation and closer definition of work was becoming evident. The improvement of roads by the Turnpike Trusts and the making of canals in the latter part of the eighteenth century made the movement of goods easier and broke down much of the dependence on purely local materials. In larger houses fashion began to have more importance and the Palladian styles of the south were being introduced by architects who themselves were becoming a recognised professional group. They could now be employed to design not only the mansion of the aristocracy but the smaller house of the yeoman. Vernacular architecture and building by the owner had passed the peak of its development and the yeoman's "long house" was to be its greatest product.

The yeoman farmers were not the only people to indulge in building during the seventeenth century. Merchants, doctors, lawyers and many of the landed families were becoming prosperous enough to desire better or more fashionable housing. In the towns of the south and particularly in London the Elizabethan styles of building had been followed by the Jacobean and Stuart of James and Charles. The Elizabethan style with its lovely mullioned windows, often with transoms, is well represented in the Dales in Friars Head at Winterburn, c. 1590, but its builder, Stephen Proctor, in 1610 built Fountains Hall in the Jacobean fashion which naturally had developed from it. The chief difference is seen in the treatment and elaboration of the doorway and the increased height of the windows. The use of the mullioned windows continued in the smaller yeoman houses throughout the seventeenth century and many larger halls like

Swinsty in the Washburn valley, Crag Hall, and the Folly at Settle, with Askrigg Hall, now unfortunately lost by fire, show developments comparable except in size with Fountains Hall. These represent the main stream of Dales building into which the new styles were injected in a few of the larger examples during the second half of the century.

The seventeenth century saw a great advance in building and also the advent of the professional architect. The first of the new architects was Inigo Jones, 1573-1652, who after travel and study in Italy and France introduced classical ideas into English building, and because of his veneration and use of the ideas of Palladio his new style became known as Palladian. The first building was the Queen's House at Greenwich, started in 1616 but after standing incomplete only finished in 1635. The Banqueting Hall in Whitehall, 1619-22, was really the type of building of the new style, and later the restoration of Old St. Pauls, 1634-43, helped to popularise the style.

The new fashions which developed from the Palladian had considerable influence later on one section of the Dales building so we must look briefly at some members of this new race of architects. Sir Christopher Wren, 1632-1723, became prominent in the rebuilding of London after the Great Fire, and retained his prominence to the end of the century. Associated with him in the building of the new St. Pauls, Greenwich Hospital, Hampton Court and other famous buildings was a young architect, Nicholas Hawksmoor, 1661-1736, who in 1700 left him to work with Sir John Vanbrugh, 1664-1726, and both had connections with the North of England. The essence of the Palladian style was the use of classical columns and details, with buildings on a large scale and often very ostentatious. It was a style suited to palaces, wealthy churches and civic buildings, and by Hawksmoor, particularly, was applied in the many University buildings of that time. Vanbrugh gave his designs size and massive grandeur but had little of the grace or delicacy of the others. His detail was often coarse and heavy. His first big work was in Yorkshire, Castle Howard, and this was a sensational building on a new scale and completely new style in 1701. Blenheim Palace followed and then back to the North at Seaton Delaval Hall. A building on a more modest scale which was to have some influence in the Dales was Linton Hospital in Wharfedale. Sir Richard Fountaine was the storybook boy who went to London, became a city alderman and died wealthy. His will of 1721 left money for an almshouse to be built in his native village of Linton and, through his London connections, Vanbrugh was selected to build it. He and Hawksmoor had already designed some almshouses for Enfield, Surrey, but these had not been built so the plans were used at Linton. Fountaine also left a substantial sum of money to the daughter of Atkinson, the owner of two very typical early seventeenth century houses in Linton—the Old Hall and what is now Linton House, both typical mullion windowed yeoman houses. She was Fountaine's niece and soon altered these two houses very much influenced by features of the new style.

The Hospital was built in a massive style which on a very small scale shows Vanbrugh's love of grandeur and heavy size which is so much evident in Castle Howard and Blenheim. The design really belongs to his Stuart and Queen Anne period and in a small way has a likeness to Morden College, Blackheath, c. 1695, which is one of his well known buildings. The Hospital has features reminding one of Palladian and others which became prominent in the Georgian. The stone was from the local Thorpe Fell quarries of Millstone Grit and the front is entirely built in massive ashlar to which this stone is so well suited. The quoins are made very prominent and the window openings have heavy surrounds. The plan is a central block which contains a chapel with an elaborate tower-surmounted entry and a cupola, the most prominent feature of the building. There is a house each side of the chapel, then a through passage to gardens at the back, and a cross wing at each end with two houses in each. The windows in the end wings have surrounds with mouldings which as Gibb's surrounds became the outstanding feature of the Georgian style, but those of the central part are built up with prominent quoins and very heavy lintels. The round headed doorway of the chapel is of fine ashlar with recessed joints. On each side of it there is a massive pillaster going right up to the parapet. The ground floor windows are the double square vertical sashes but the first floor windows are a single square with Yorkshire sliding sash. This building which is worth close study later inspired the Atkinson niece to alter her two houses. The Old Hall had one end replaced by a three storey Georgian extension with an excellent pedimented doorway and good windows with moulded surrounds, while a new very well proportioned Georgian house was built onto the front of the seventeenth century Linton House. So it is that Stuart, Palladian and Georgian styles came into this part of the Dales and were later copied in some nearby villages. Fine Georgian houses can be seen in Cracoe, Rilston and Thorpe, and Grassington House, built about 1760 by Mr. Brown, a promoter of the Grassington to Pateley Bridge Turnpike road, is in an excellent Georgian style. There is also a good Georgian house to be seen at Yockenthwaite at the head of the valley.

The Palladian and its Vanbrugh modification had its latest northern enthusiast in the Earl of Burlington, 1694-1753, whose best known work was the Assembly Rooms in York. William Kemp, 1685-1748, born at Rotherham, also used the Palladian type but like Vanbrugh made changes leading towards the

Georgian which flourished in the eighteenth century after 1714. In the North of England two architects were active from time to time in Dales building, John Carr of York, 1723-1807, and John Foss of Richmond, 1745-1827. John Carr started out as a Palladian enthusiast but was influenced by the Gothic revival and developed his own northern version of it. He was the son of a small quarry owner who also worked as mason contractor and builder, and John worked with his father until he was thirty-seven. His father was superintendent of the building at Harewood House for which John was the architect. He was also the architect of Wentworth Woodhouse, Denton Hall and some other large houses, as well as working for a time with the Earl of Burlington.

In the second half of the eighteenth century the urge towards the larger country house, which had swept the south of the country, reached the North along with much of the Palladian classic tradition and Carr took advantage of this. One of the earliest houses where this can be seen is Marske Hall in Swaledale. This was entirely rebuilt in the 1750s in a modified Palladian style, which is seen in the severe classical lines, symmetrical façade and the importance given to the entry with its classical columns and pediment. In 1761 Charles Turner of Kirkleatham commissioned Carr to alter Clints Hall which he had just bought. This is very near Marske Hall and Carr gave it a classical entrance in the middle of the old façade, as at Marske but with pedimented windows on each side. In 1762 one of Carr's larger designs, the rebuilding of Constable Burton in a pure Palladian form, began and was not completed until 1768. This was his last purely Palladian work characterised by a massive portico of classical columns with a triangular pediment above it, and severe rectangular and symmetrical front. In 1764 Turner had asked him to rebuild Kirkleatham Hall and this he did in the next three years. This was one of the earliest houses in the North of England to be built in what was the new fashion of the so-called Gothic revival. The taste for Gothic had spread rapidly among the country families and was soon to become popular in the North. Carr devised his own version of Gothic and used this in his alterations at Ripley Castle in 1781. At Ripley also can be seen the interest which Carr had in the Georgian style which was beginning to influence much Dales building.

John Foss of Richmond was a local architect who did much work which has survived. His largest building is the very striking Swinton Castle, part a rebuilding but mostly an extension onto an older house. This romantic looking castle was a break away from the severe Palladian into something largely fanciful. The work was done about 1820. Before this in 1792 he had built the very impressive Swinnithwaite Hall in Wensleydale. It is of fine ashlar walling with a five bay front in which he has included the Palladian detail of a pedimented doorway and a Venetian window, though the general feeling is a restrained Georgian. Clifton Castle was built in 1802 with more Palladian about it. Many other mansions, Aske Hall and Hornby Castle among them, were considerably extended or partly rebuilt in the first half of the nineteenth century, either hiding or in some cases replacing the older halls and manors. These buildings however are all alien to the Dales traditional building and their position and place is with the architectural fashions of the country at large.

A reflection of the new fashions in building was seen in some smaller houses—not cottages, but houses that were being built for a middle class which was emerging. Professional men, doctors, lawyers, clergy and the merchant traders, particularly in the towns but also in some villages, were seeking better or more fashionable homes. In the cities like York a new type of house was replacing the long and very narrow houses which extended back some distance from the street along narrow alleyways and yards. This new style, soon called Georgian, had houses with a generous square plan, wide front and, when possible, free-standing, clear of its neighbours and perhaps with a garden at the rear. The simplest plan for the smaller house was four approximately equal rooms on the ground floor: two rooms, the dining room and drawing room, at the front, and service rooms—a kitchen and scullery or small rooms—at the back. A fine staircase rising from the hall separated the rooms and might be an interesting feature, and was on the centre line of the house. Four rooms on the first floor corresponded with those below—the attics were appropriated to the servants and stores. Plumbing was minimal; servants carried water for washstands, and baths and commodes supplemented a ground floor cloakroom-toilet. The proportions used in the new houses were the greatest innovation. Rooms were made as near as possible to the cube and so were much higher than in the earlier houses. Higher rooms meant higher windows and the typical Georgian is the double square sash window in a heavy surround of cut stone monolithic jambs, lintel and sill, usually with a slight moulding and projecting a little from the wall face. Quoins also projected a little and the whole walling was in smooth finished ashlar. These windows and quoin features in ashlar had already been introduced by Vanbrugh in the Linton Hospital and copied in other buildings.

There were usually five or nine windows to the front, or even thirteen, arranged symmetrically, one, two or three each side of the door and then one extra window above the door. A hipped roof was occasionally used but in the Dales the straight gabled roof seemed more appropriate. The doorway was always made a prominent feature, the frame being similar to those of the windows but crowned with a protruding heavy pediment either triangular or segmental. These houses stand out wherever they occur, very attractive in their own right but having a "towny" appearance among the plainer building of a village. Adaptations of all the Georgian features, but especially the square plan with rooms two deep, were made for larger as well as for smaller houses and soon became the common town housing type.

The very attractive Georgian style of the eighteenth century architects was soon taken up by the rural builder and, in a countryfied form, spread through the Dales so that many villages have houses of Georgian plan and a façade which is Georgian in its proportions, distribution of windows and door, and in its prominent quoins, but all the detail is in the simplest possible form. The windows of Georgian sash proportions are made without surrounds and with walled sides, a plain sill and a lintel with little or no moulding but perhaps with a thin flag over it. The door jambs will be of lean proportion with a simple fillet round the outer side and a moulded cornice instead of the more elaborate pediment. Quoins are not likely to be chamfered and may not stand proud of the wall. Nonetheless these are not so much poor relations of the best Georgian tradition as they are the rural appreciation of the style and its adaptation to the frugal means and inclination of the countryman and his builder.

In dwindling size and further elimination of detail which is non-functional, this became the plan and pattern of the nineteenth century larger cottage dwelling—two "front rooms", kitchen and scullery, with the living room and parlour at the front and the service rooms behind. A smaller cottage was made with little fuss by halving this—two bedrooms, kitchen-living room and back scullery-wash place which provided bath room and anything else needed. In the villages the uniformity of the town row was never possible and the monotony of the style was avoided. Spaces varied and nearly every cottage was an individual job capable of small variations, and such variation within narrow limits was nearly always achieved. In addition to this cottage type every village has had its individual with his own ideas, and so there are buildings which cannot be fitted into any regular plan or type but which add a spice and seasoning of originality.

The artisan and labouring population was expanding during the eighteenth and nineteenth centuries and groups like the miners in the northern dales were almost equalling the farm labourers in numbers. For the mines in particular many new families were brought from other areas. There are many families still in the Dales which came from Derbyshire in the seventeenth or eighteenth century, some from Alston Moor and some even from Cornwall. Mining populations have traditionally moved to other areas in times of depression and also when prosperity comes to a new area. This immigration as well as natural increase made a great demand for housing. As always in such cases employers, landlords and the people themselves tried to meet the demand by the quickest, cheapest and most expedient methods. Some old hovels were patched up or rebuilt but many remained in use until a late date. Plantagenet Harrison writing in the Gilling area in 1885 says: "I remember ... about 55 years ago (1830) a few very ancient haggs, houses built of turf and thatched with straw ... but they have recently been replaced by a row of stone cottages." Much of the rebuilding and new building was infilling on the tofts, on part of which old cottages had been built, so that stretches of continuously built up village street were created. This is why in many villages houses of all kinds and sizes are mixed together, and whatever their quality their variety gives interest and charm to the scene.

It was rare for labouring families to have the means with which to build their own house and in this situation the jobbing builder found his proper place. Cottages were in demand and a simple traditional plan of two rooms side by side and two rooms above, needing only a narrow roof, was easy and cheap to build. One fireplace, a door opening direct into the fireplace room, often near the gable wall on which was the chimney, was sufficient and a family or a family and lodger was often able to be moderately comfortable though overcrowded in these houses. It was not long before many cottages of this kind were being built with the minimum of elaboration or variety. Windows on the ground floor were sashes, no longer of Georgian proportions but much lower, and for the bedrooms kept as low as possible with a sash of Yorkshire type, sliding horizontally when an opening window was desired.

With the great multiplication of labourers' cottages the labouring part of the population became almost entirely a rent paying population and the ties within the village community were weakened. Families moved more easily in times of depression and found refuge in the growing towns. The local born proportion became less. The cottages of this eighteenth and nineteenth century infilling have little individual merit, but most of them have by now weathered into their position as part of the village scene and are more acceptable than the bowed and picture windows, fancy doors and pseudo Tudor hinges, coach or gas lamps and other evidences of towny taste which have been imposed as "improvements" in the last few years. These give urgency to a stricter planning control if the character of our villages is not to be eroded in a flood of uninformed suburban "taste".

This book is concerned entirely with a rural area where the unit of aggregation is the village and where we can ignore the town. Even our "market towns", Hawes, Leyburn, Sedbergh, are only larger villages. We say the overall view of most Dales villages is attractive, pleasing, something worth looking at and frequently photographed and painted. And yet look closely and critically, one by one at the houses and other buildings in any village, and only a minority, a very few, are of special merit. Most seen in isolation would not provoke comment or a closer look. What is the quality then that makes the assembled village attractive? It is surely more psychological than material. The buildings outstanding as well as insignificant are mixed together in no particular order but just as they have been made in response to some need. Many of the cottages would look mean if seen in the long repetition of a town street. In the village they are part of the community's dwelling place as their tenants are or were part of the community known for the job they were doing, whether it were doctor, craftsman, farmer or labourer. It is this visible evidence of a village community, its houses clustered together in close neighbourhood, growing from the materials and traditions of the area, that gives the village a unity and a character. It is this character which is sensitive to town fashion intrusions when cottages are "improved" to please only a new owner with little reference to the character of all its neighbours. Ostentation has been singularly rare in the vernacular tradition —most people could not afford it—and when it is introduced, particularly in the "second home" which is only used for holidays and weekends, and has no reference to the working life of the village, it becomes an intrusion. A very present problem is that of persuading this new element now coming into every village to accept a modest place in the community with understanding and perception which can recognise the characteristics of the village life and not try to impose town fashions upon it. This is not a plea for dead uniformity but for understanding and avoidance of arrogance, and perhaps also a plea to leave behind the gaslamp standard, the distinguishing primary coloured door and also the cement-wash colour card of suburbia.

The rise in prosperity and status of the yeoman farmer in the eighteenth century which came with the beginning of the Enclosures led to the creation of the new farm with buildings gathered round a yard and no longer added to the end of a house already long enough. Some barns and shippons were added to those which already by old tradition were out in the fields, but these were old and kept to traditional size and form having usually the hay from one meadow and with standings for only two or three beasts. There is some excellent building to be found among these and variations which give each dale its own recognisable character. Buildings near the farm house were larger and more frequently separated functionally. Hay barns and shippons were often separated in a way now represented by the food store and the milking parlour. For one or two generations the farmer gave more attention to his farm buildings than to his house, the turn of which was delayed to the late nineteenth or even the early twentieth century.

Arthur Young had been touring the North of England and the journal of this, *Six Months Tour in the North of England*, was published in 1770 and was a prelude to the County surveys of the Board of Agriculture which came at the end of the century. In this he commented on farm improvements, both those which he saw and those he recommended. Arthur Young's *Tour* was in no way like many other eighteenth century tours—it was a detailed description of the state of agriculture with a full note of any practice which he thought to be good. He gave a critical assessment of any new and experimental methods which he saw being operated and wrote and intended it for the use and instruction of farmers throughout the country. Knowing that most of the small farmers would not be able to read his book, he addressed it to the larger farmers and country landowners who might apply some of the advice on their estates. For their benefit he gave much advice and among that which mainly concerned the management of land, crops and stock, he included from time to time advice on designing and building farm properties. He was very careful to collect prices in almost every place he visited and these he set out in tables as the cost of food, wages and, from time to time, implements and building materials. Among prices quoted for the Yorkshire Dales, it will be of interest to some readers to have a few examples as information on things such as he gives is comparatively rare. Among others he gives the prices for building combined with advice on the buildings required for a new farm to replace an old one, most of those he saw in the Dales being thought by him to be old and inefficient. His advice was to some extent taken on the larger estates like those of Swinton, Kirkleatham, Danby and Ripley.

He suggested that the minimum farm should, besides a good dwelling, have a large barn, stables, cowhouse and hogsties, preferably ranged round an enclosed yard. He says that in the Dales farms should be built of stone and slate, and this suggests that possibly there were still many survivals of timber framed and thatched cruck buildings. He describes and prices a farm which was then being built near Danby, without suggesting its plan. The dimensions of the house and stable can be derived by careful study and they agree very well with those of the traditional four bayed house. He makes matters a little difficult by taking as his basic dimension for a building, its *circumference*. However, as internal division walls are mentioned the others are easily calculated. It appears that the house he described was 14 ft. wide and 63 ft. long inside, allowing 2 ft. walls. The two partition walls are 14 ft. long and 18 ft. high to the base of the triangular gable which is of 14 ft. base and 12 ft. high. This would give the common pitch for a thatched roof. With two internal walls the house was one of three rooms. One, the two bayed one, would be the kitchen-living room—in our colloquial wording, the "house" —and the others would be parlour and dairy. The two fireplaces would most likely be back to back on a party wall.

His comments, prices and descriptions include some information on the largest of our built monuments, the vast network of stone walls that clothes the whole of our countryside. It is so much a part of our landscape that it is taken for granted and not noticed except by the curious stranger. Mr. Scrope of Danby had taken in 900 acres of rough moor and began its enclosure and improvement; he first cleared and started to wall. We cannot do better than quote Young's own words:

"His first business was the enclosure which he did by walling; the surface of the moor yielded in some places, a sufficiency of stones for this work, but in many other pits were sunk for them, the quarries are all limestone, and mostly near the surface. The first year 289 roods were built of the ring fence. This work was all contracted for by the measure, at 5s. 6d. a rood, of seven yards long, and five feet high. A gate and two posts, and the irons, came to 6s."

This is a picture which can be applied to many parts of the Dales and anyone walking alongside the moorland walls can still see scores of these grass grown "walling quarries".

"At the same time that this business was carrying on, the foundations of a farmhouse and offices were laid; But as something more than a slight account of these improvements is here meant, it will be useful to minute the size and expence of these buildings, that false ideas of the expence of improving uncultivated lands may not become more common than they are already.

The house was 170 feet in circumference by 18 feet high, or 234 superficial yards. The gables, above the line, 18 by 14 or 28 superficial yards. Two partition-walls, 14 by 18 each or 56 superficial yards. Partition gable 14 by 12 or 18 yards.

The circumference of the stable was 80 feet by 11 high, or 97 superficial yards. Gable tops 16 by 12, or 21 yards.

In both, 455 yards at 6d. per yard, workmanship; the wall 22 inches thick	£11. 7.6
Two chimneys to the first floor	1.10.0
Ditto, the second floor	1. 1.0
Edging the gables, called windskews	0. 7.6
An oven	0. 8.0
36 Quoit-stones, at 3d.	0. 9.0
6 Windows, and door-stead 105 feet, at 5d.	3. 4.7
Door and window-stead in stable 40 at 5d.	0.16.8
Sundry small articles	0.15.2

19.19.5

Two cart load of stones of three yards; the getting costs 2d. per load
and the carriage 2d., this is 2½d. per yard, on 455 yards 4.15.0

£24.14.5

For now, the house and set of offices being finished, and preparations being
made for the walling and improving, by opening several quarries both for
the walls and burning of lime, the grand work will go on fast: the old team
respited from attending the buildings, and the new ones being also free, both
will be employed by the walling and tillage alone.''

The roof is mentioned separately:

"If the roof is thatch the carpenter's work is 2s. per square for hewing,
sawing, and joining, the spars only rived poles. Thatching the roof of a barn
9 square and 80 feet; and a granary, 5 square and 52 feet, cost £5 2s. If the
roof is slated, the carpenter's work is then, for hewing, sawing and joining
6s. a square. A rood of 49 superficial yards of slating costs
The slates at quarry, £1 12s. 0d. Carriage, four miles £0 7s. 0d., laying
on, £1 1s. 0d.—£3 0s. 0d."

This account seems very cheap but it must be remembered
that the whole of the stone was got as land clearance. If it had
been bought at the quarry as most building in the dale would
have had to do, then the cost would have been very much greater.
The costs of building a barn in Craven can be seen in accounts
submitted to the Earl of Thanet. An old barn of much greater
size than the stables that Young itemises, and perhaps equalling
the house, show an interesting comparison. The blacksmith's
accounts for nails alone was £2 2s. 6½d. Pulling down old building
£3 10s. 0d., rewalling with old stone 3s. 9d. a yard, but new
walling 6s. 0d. a rood. Slating was 12s. 0d. a rood, 18 tons of
slate cost 9s. 6d. a ton, barn floor flags 1s. 0d. a yard, and house
floor flags 10d. The total cost of a barn with chamber and
housing for a hind at one end, with bought stone, slates and
flags, and with Bradford stone and ashlar for tabling and other
special parts, all internal fittings included, comes to £64 12s. 10d.
Using both accounts we can get some sort of idea of the cost
of building at the latter quarter of the eighteenth century, the
two accounts being 1770 and 1788 respectively. Several other
accounts, some complete and some only fragments, agree well
with these pricings.

All the available documents go to support the idea that most
of the larger farm buildings were either replacements or extensions to farms in the approximate half century of the 1770s to
1820s or '30s and that this was the time when the farm yards
surrounded by the buidings were adopted as the general farm
plan.

7. Social and Industrial Buildings

A COMPLETE account of Dales building would have to include a number of isolated buildings which might be classed as social or industrial. Each village usually has one or more but they lie for the most part entirely outside local building tradition; they are connected with some aspect of the community life or some sectional interest. Perhaps the most obvious and widespread are the chapels. With the rise of Non-conformity the parish churches, which in any case served a parish of many townships and villages and were central to a large area, were abandoned by members of the new sects. For some time in the seventeenth century Quakers and Independents had their meetings in houses or barns, but with the eighteenth century—when Wesley visited the Dales and had great conversions among the miners and labourers—the communities became too large for house meetings. In the nineteenth century most of the chapels were built—the Quaker meeting houses were earlier. Meeting houses and chapels at first were very plain simple buildings, functional and built usually without an architect and often by the voluntary labour of the congregation. Of the Friends (Quaker) meeting houses the one at Countersett is in Dales traditional style, but that at Carperby is more in the later Georgian form. As congregations grew in strength and resources, new chapels were built by architects who adopted a hybrid Gothicism which they thought necessary to emphasise a place of religion and the resultant building is often alien to every other in its village. They are accepted by present viewers because such a building is expected. It would only be possible to describe these buildings individually and that is not within the scope of this book. Very few recent buildings of schools, institutes, housing and so on have much relation to local traditions of building, so these too will not be dealt with here.

There are a few industrial buildings which can be mentioned as worthy of note. Most villages had a corn mill located on the stream within or near to the village and a regular contributor to the routine of village life. These are no longer in use, though a few remain. A few villages were affected by the Industrial

Revolution which brought cotton manufacture into the area. In its early years this used the water power of the rivers and streams and needed the new form of building, the mill.

The water corn mills, often dating from the twelfth or thirteenth century, had a single pair of stones but with a permanent right to the use of the water or river near which they were built. In later centuries they were enlarged or rebuilt with two or more pairs of stones and larger water wheels. At least two of these mills remain, Bainbridge and Fremington, neither of them now working but retaining all their grinding machinery. When flour became available from the local markets, coming from the large steam driven mills at the ports which processed imported corn, the small local mills fell out of use. Their water rights continued and in many cases these were taken over and the mills altered to be used for the new invented textile processes. During the second half of the eighteenth century many small corn mills with a good water supply were rebuilt for cotton spinning. A fine example of such a mill built on an old site is the one on the side of Gayle Beck, immediately below the village. This three storey, six bay mill was built in 1784 for the cotton trade, but has later served for both flax and wool spinning, and now is part joiners' sawmill and part building stores. Another fine early mill is Grassington Low Mill on the bank of the river Wharfe, but fed by a powerful underground stream which only comes to light a few yards behind the mill. It is on the site of an early corn mill but in turn has been used for cotton, silk and flax spinning, for soap making, then furniture, and now converted to house property. The mill at Aysgarth Bridge, Yore Mill, has a curious reversion in its uses. Built in 1784 for cotton spinning it became in turn a woollen spinning mill, making yarn for stocking knitters, making blankets and knitted jerseys. Rebuilt after destruction by fire in 1853, it later became a corn grinding and provender storage concern, and now is a coach and carriage museum. Arncliffe Mill followed a comparable pattern, cotton, silk, woollens, with more than one rebuilding, and finally houses. In these and other mills, steam power supplemented the water power at a late date. These mills were built in the new way, by building contractors.

These are only a few of the many mills which in the nineteenth century were numerous in the Dales. In Swaledale the largest of them all was only recently demolished, that at Haverdale on Crackpot Beck. Of those at Askrigg, the Low Mill has been altered to social uses, and two at Hawes are among the few survivors, though like others changed in usage. Dentdale had several mills, and around Sedbergh there was the big mill at Birks, one at Millthrop and one in the mouth of Garsdale at Farfield. The one at Hebblethwaite is now only seen as slight ruins. Nearly all started as cotton spinning mills but changed to woollens. In Nidderdale the several mills were concerned with flax spinning, the best remaining structure being that of Foster Beck with its outside water wheel preserved as an attraction for visitors.

Apart from their industrial history, these mills are a part of the building history of many of our villages and were large enough to help the establishment of small firms of building contractors during the nineteenth century. Wheelwrights, foundrymen and engineers employed in fitting up the mills mostly came from towns just outside the Dales, like Skipton, Stockton and Kendal.

One other industry, older and larger than that of textiles, has left a few evidences of local building skill, most of the building about the mines being done by the masons normally employed there. The work which is seldom seen is the several miles of fine masonry arching lining some of the mine levels, but work employing the same skill is to be seen in the flues which climb up the hillsides from some of the smelting mills. The flues are now in bad repair, some like that from Keld Head mill collapsed for much of their length, but great lengths of some are still complete. The system of flues from the Cupola on Grassington Moor is nearly complete and terminates in a fine tall chimney on the moor top. Flues can also be seen at Grinton, Surrender and Old Gang mills in Swaledale and in Arkengarthdale the flues from the Langthwaite mill can be seen in sections spread over a mile of hillside. There are still chimneys at Malham Moor, Starbotton and Hurst, and parts of chimneys at Old Gang, Surrender, Cobscar and the base of chimneys at other mills.

For the smelting large quantities of peat were used and the peat houses built for its storage were sometimes of great size and special construction. The sides were often a long arcade of open arches to allow the peat to dry, and the largest of all of them is that at Old Gang. Others remain at Surrender and Blakethwaite, and more ordinary houses at Grinton and Keld Heads. Other buildings special to ore dressing are also frequent in the mining field, and all are a testimony to the skill of the mine masons who not only did the building but usually quarried the stone as well.

Like the smaller domestic buildings, the industrial buildings are a testimony to the craft of the local masons and builders who in many cases were their own quarrymen and architects. Some of the mill properties are contributing a new element to Dales housing and the essentially town habit of flat dwelling is being introduced. The large mill at Airton in Airedale has now been converted into a number of quite roomy flats, most of which will be "second homes" accommodation. This has been done successfully while preserving the external appearance of this dignified Victorian mill. Grassington and Arncliffe mills in Wharfedale have been converted to domestic housing and other mills have been similarly altered. Low Mill at Askrigg has very recently been converted into a very attractive hostel for field studies, to be used by children from Leeds and Bradford. This movement which is preserving what is left of the mills is very welcome, as they have played a most important part in the economic life of the villages and were responsible for some of the infilling cottages of the nineteenth century.

A feature of the increasing settlement of newcomers into the Dales is the large number of conversions of old buildings, especially farm buildings, barns and shippons, now displaced by the far more obtrusive prefabricated structures. Some of these conversions have been well done within the spirit of the Dales building traditions. Only a few have tried to bring town fashions to brighten up and bring "up to date" what the new owners appear to regard as a backward rural scene. New buildings must have aroused criticism ever since the first Norman Castle was built and possibly before that, but such criticism if it is informed, sympathetic and logical is a good and acceptable ingredient in our community life.

Further Reading

On the subject of building in the Dales there is very little literature. The background and a little general discussion will be found in the following: —

Raistrick, A., Articles in *The Dalesman*, vol. 3, 1941-42.

Walton, J., *Homesteads of the Yorkshire Dales*, Dalesman, 1947.

Raistrick, A., *Old Yorkshire Dales*, Newton Abbot, 1967.

Raistrick, A., *Pennine Dales*, London; particularly chapters 6, 8 and 9.

For the work and organisation of masons, quarrymen and carpenters there are a few excellent books:

Coulton, G. C., *Art in the Reformation*, Oxford, 1928, has several chapters on buildings and on masons.

Knoop, D. & Jones, G. P., *The Medieval Mason*, Manchester University Press, 1933.

Salzman, L. F., *Building in England down to 1540*, Oxford University Press, 1952.

The structure of buildings using crucks and timber is most fully described in:

Addy, S. O., *The evolution of the English house*, 1898, reprinted 1933.

Innocent, C. F., *The Development of English Building Construction*, Cambridge University Press, 1916, reprint David & Charles, 1971.

These are both mainly concerned with the Sheffield-Huddersfield districts. Walton, J., has several papers in the Yorkshire Archaeological Journal on cruck building.

Braun, H., *The Story of the English House*, London, 1940, is very good, though mostly discussing examples from the Midlands and South. A book by Barley, M. W., *The English farmhouse and cottage*, London, 1961, ought to be read but it is mainly concerned with the plan, accommodation and furnishing and says little or nothing about the actual building methods. It deals with houses to 1725 and has no reference to the Dales except to quote one Cracoe document. Brunskill, R. W., *Illustrated handbook to vernacular architecture*, 1970, is a useful reference book to the architectural detail of the smaller houses.

The best source of study is still to be found in looking carefully at buildings in the Dales—nothing can replace this careful field work.